P9-AQC-727

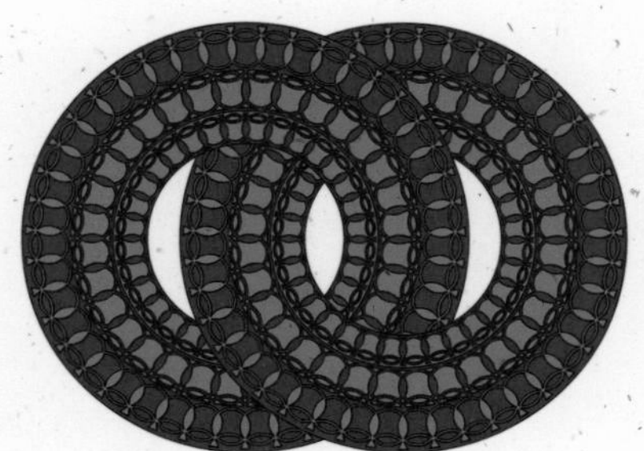

THE *POETRY* LIFE

BARON WORMSER

TEN STORIES

THE *POETRY* LIFE

BARON WORMSER

TEN STORIES

5.08
Maine

For Pat,
In the poetry life,
Baron

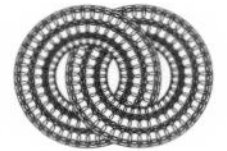

CavanKerry Press LTD.

CavanKerry Press Ltd.
Fort Lee, New Jersey
www.cavankerrypress.org

Library of Congress Cataloging-in-Publication Data

Wormser, Baron.
The Poetry life : ten stories / Baron Wormser. – 1st ed.
p. cm.
ISBN-13: 978-1-933880-05-1
ISBN-10: 1-933880-05-8
I. Title.

PS3573.O693P64 2008
813'.54–dc22

2007038839

Cover art by James O'Brien © 2007, Author photograph by Maisie Wormser, Cover and book design by Peter Cusack

First Edition 2008, Printed in the United States of America

NOTABLE VOICES

CavanKerry Press is proud to publish the works
of established poets of merit and distinction.

CavanKerry Press is grateful for the support it
receives from the New Jersey State Council on the Arts.

Thanks to the following for their support: Willard Spiegelman, Mary Cotton, Ellen Dudley, George Core, Jill Patterson, Ryan Walsh, Donna McNeil, the Vermont Studio Center, Richard Miles, Sally Read, Candice Stover, Shaun Griffin, Ann Hood, Robin Talbot, Dawn Potter, Florenz Eisman, Peter Cusack, Joan Handler, and my dear, acute wife Janet.

Grateful acknowledgment is made to the editors and publishers of the following publications in which these stories first appeared under the following titles:

Southwest Review, "William Blake"
Sewanee Review, "Weldon's Song"
Post Road, "John Berryman, b. 1914"
Marlboro Review, "Anne Sexton"
Iron Horse Literary Review, "Audre Lorde"

"William Blake" was awarded a 2006 McGinnis-Ritchie Award for Fiction from the *Southwest Review*.

For three poets:

Jeanne Marie Beaumont, Philip Fried, Andrey Gritsman

Contents

THE *POETRY* LIFE

BARON WORMSER

TEN STORIES

William Blake, b.1757

I rise before the sun does. Each morning I sit on the edge of the bed with my feet planted on the unlovely linoleum floor and I say slowly but quite distinctly to the darkness, "Sweet joy befall thee." I feel like an actor speaking the first words of a play except my life is no play nor does my soul need an audience. What I do need is confidence. I've built my life up from very shaky ground and William Blake, the man who wrote that line, has been a godsend to me. The human voice that speaks a poem rises from a powerful well; we take it for granted but a voice is an advent of spirit. I know from attending numerous churches during my haphazard childhood that the joy that preachers trumpet comes in a box with grievous dimensions. Their salvation is a machine of wrath; they break your back on hell so you can get to heaven. The joy I invoke can go where it chooses because it resides in our being alive. The joy I invoke is Blake's Jerusalem, the city we can build each day through kindness: "The most sublime act is to set another before you." No one has ever called the place where I work "sublime," so I need that word, too.

Those words I speak do not constitute a prayer. They are somewhere between an announcement and a wish. I know if left to its own devices my daily mind will kick in about whether I remembered to get cat food or whether my beater of a car will start or whether I will be walking down the street, and the pain of my wondering who my parents were will hit me out of nowhere like quiet lightning and I will tingle with grief. Repeating that line of poetry takes me to my soul's desire. Whatever I am to myself and to others—aide at a home for retarded folks, spiritualist, would-be poet, wandering orphan—I reside on the same earth that my master William Blake once walked on. He saw the sky and sun that I see. He knew they were spiritual emanations. He recognized the glory that refutes despair and dwarfs knowledge. Despair has been near my heart forever; I don't use the word lightly.

To study something—the sky or the sun or a lamb or a house fly—in the way that our scientific world likes to study things is to sever your heart from your mind. The people with whom I work are studied endlessly. Questions fly from educated mouths: How did they get to be this way? What pills could make them better? What is "better"? What do their brains look like? It's easy to forget that those modest brains belong to people. It's easy to forget that those "objective" scientists are people themselves. Before we do anything with anything we should exult that it exists. The belief that everything is explicable frightens me. When human beings start to explain, they reduce eternity to a shoe size. Eternity, to quote Blake, is in love with the productions of time, not the explanations of time.

Children come to recognize that an explanation delivered in the voice of authority is a lie. I know I did when a foster parent explained to me why I had to be going to another house next week when I had barely gotten used to being in the house I was in. Those reasons adults trot out are convenient ways to silence the large and small questions a child raises. Practicality cannot be bothered. The child looking up at the harried adult who cannot make ends meet and has forgotten (or never known) what love might be senses what lies within an explanation. The voice that the child hears is truly "half-hearted;" it is only part of a heart, not a whole one.

I am glad to work with "slow" people because they insist on asking the large and small questions. They will ask with great curiosity what is for lunch and then they will wonder aloud as we amble down the hall toward the day room why the sun came up today. What explanation do I have for them? "Because it loves you," I say. They smile and are happy to accept fondness. "Every thing possible to be believed is an image of truth." I know these "slow" people know that.

I know, too, that the chimney sweeps in Blake's London also rose early. They moved from one darkness to another, as they made their way from the sleep that was their only refuge (though I cringe to think of their nightmares) into the narrow, suffocating, smoky chimneys. Five-, six-, seven-year-olds, they lived to be used up as if they were wood and coal. How fallen a world it is that treats flesh as if it were a material, that humbles beauty and applauds blindness. Slavery changes its coats according to fashion but it swears the same hard, necessitous oaths. Its easy words remain fanatical; its consolations murderous—work will make us free, honor the rod that beats you, die for the honor of a nation. Those common, preening lies angered Blake; he lamented but he clung to his vision. While I dress and attend to Tiger, Los, and Crystal who are milling around my legs and meowing, I often think of Blake's poem. Sometimes I say a stanza to myself:

> And by came an Angel who had a bright key,
> And he opened the coffins & set them all free;
> Then down a green plain leaping, laughing, they run,
> And wash in a river, and shine in the Sun.

I'm not an angel but I hope each day that I have "a bright key." I work the seven to three at the Hill and Dale Manor. That word "Manor" covers a multitude of possibilities. It's one pretentious step up from Residence, which also covers many bases. A Residence could be a place for recovering alcoholics or homeless people or some other population that has nowhere else to reside. There are a lot of populations like that, with old people forming the biggest one. They move slowly, old people, and get in the way. I think that's how the world at large looks at them. Younger people don't seem to feel that some day they will become unwanted old people. As for old retarded people, they move even more slowly and are even more in the way. That's why they are housed in Hill and Dale Manor where they can be slow together and not cramp the world that needs to be running faster and faster. When someone asks me what I do, I say that I take care of slow people who are moving slowly. I get a funny look when I say that but it's true. I tell whoever has asked me that moving slowly is the way to go. You appreciate life more when you take time. We know that death is out there; there's no point in hurrying. Old Reuben Thompson can take most of the morning going down the hall. He pauses for very long times and God only knows what he thinks or sees. He rarely speaks. The official designation is "catatonic" but that doesn't tell you much you couldn't observe for yourself. He probably hears voices but so did William Blake.

The largest numbers of people who live where I work are classified as retarded, meaning "backward in mental or physical development." The official words to describe them seem to change every six months but that particular word is good enough. We try to paper over cruelty and what we perceive as misfortune with words. Somehow the well-meaning words that avoid the thoughtless words are supposed to make us feel better, as if a bland word could make suffering go away, as if indifference could summon kindness. Those bureaucratic words make me feel worse. I think, in part, that's why poems exist. They peel the word-paper off and let you feel language as it wants to be felt—vital and unapologetic as an animal.

Our director gets into a considerable dither about whether we are using the right words. The state shows up now and then to look at our paperwork and see whether we are operating according to the hundreds of rules and regulations they have. Language is part of the drill, as if words on paper affected how people are treated. Would that it were that simple. Hypocrisy, double-dealing, and contempt are not on the state's map. If you say the most correct, neutral word then everything will be okay. They are well-intentioned liberals, the sort of people who drove Blake crazy with their know-it-all assurance. "The crow wished every thing was black; the owl that every thing was white." So Blake wrote and so these good people want the ungainly world to conform to their mental vision. I've been known to roll my eyes to my fellow employees when state inspectors start asking us questions. Doreen, the Manor's social director, sticks out her tongue behind their backs. It's not very grown up but I don't see them hanging around to clean up the pee, shit, drool, and vomit. Maybe I should use some words next time to help clean up.

The people who make these messes are "clients." I doubt if any of them would recognize the word. They sure don't get up in the morning and say, "Well, here I am, a client." I'm trying to teach some of them to say "Sweet joy befall thee" when they rise but it's an uphill climb. "Befall" is a hard word to get around a cumbrous tongue. Plus they don't tend toward standard, recognizable English. They have their own takes on language. What at first were to me a bunch of grunts and wheezes have turned out to be commands and thoughts and feelings. Sally Whitehead, who's been there forever and acts as though she was born yesterday, will look directly at me and stutter a string of sounds that mostly are the letter *m*. Depending on how long she looks at me and how calm or agitated she is and how quickly she speaks, I have a sense of whether she wants help with a button or to take a walk or she thinks it's a beautiful day. Some state inspector might tell me I'm making it all up but I don't think so. When I do what she wants, she purrs like a cat.

Calling the place where I work a "Manor" is one of those bad jokes that pretension never seems to tire of. Most of the help calls the place the "Minor." That's how the help usually is; they see the truth and speak it. They know that you can make good money seeing to the needs of the retarded. The owner, Jake DeRoche, spends most of the year playing golf in Florida. Retardation has been good to him. He doesn't know I exist because when he does appear he only speaks to the director. She's usually so distracted from the paperwork and the help not showing up when they're supposed to because a car's broken or a boyfriend's left or a kid's sick and so subservient to her boss that she swoons whenever he sets foot in the place.

I've seen him a few times and he's become a figure in my pantheon of evil spirits. Blake, you recall, had many such figures. I've done some drawings of Jake but he's too bland to have that Old Testament feeling Blake gave to his bad guys. There's no flowing beard or angry eyes. He's more like an overfilled Twinkie. He's got a potbelly, puts some kind of grease on his hair, even though he doesn't have much hair to begin with, and he spits when he talks—the way some of the "clients" do. He has that awful smile of people who think they have everything figured out. He's on top of the world with his condo in Florida and his new Cadillac every other year and his who-knows-how-much-they-cost shoes but if you ask me he's all bottled up inside and what's in there is festering. He's been walking in the wrong direction for a long time and the world has been telling him it's the right direction. You could say that Jesus would have pitied him but I think Jesus would have said, "Wake up, buddy, and see how you are treating people."

Someone told me that he gets real angry on the golf course when he misses a putt. Someone told me he cheats. He sure isn't spending a fortune on the Minor or on my non-union salary. But then the people who live in his so-called manor are retards and I'm spending my spare time reading William Blake when I could be taking business administration courses at the local college and getting a grip on how I can get ahead. Imagine thinking that money measures anything about human beings. What a strange thought.

One of the beauties of the people with whom I work is that they are indifferent to money. When we play bingo (and we do most days), we play for pennies. To not care about money is almost unbelievable. It shows how totally out of it you are. To me it seems the other way around. Money stands squarely in the middle of the road for each of us and blocks the human way. We walk over it or around it or retreat or try to blow it up or bury it but in any case we know money is there and we can't escape it. As Jake the director shows, having a lot of money doesn't mean you stop thinking about money. On the contrary, you become money. Every moment translates into what it will cost and what you will make. What the people here want are very simple pleasures—eating freshly popped popcorn, playing cards, watching their favorite TV shows. No wonder the world forthrightly used to refer to them as idiots. Only an idiot forgets about money.

I know that William Blake had to pay his bills and that I have to pay mine. I'm sure he lay in bed sometimes and worried about how he was going to make his next buck. I'm sure he envied painters and printmakers who made the money he didn't make. If you're an adult and you're wired up the regular way adults are, then you can't ignore money. The mates (my abbreviation of "inmates" though everyone thinks it's nautical) are wired up differently; they have remained children of a sort. Like children they connect directly with the world around them, a world that gives them more than money ever could. "To create a little flower is the labor of ages." Children intuit that. It's why Blake wrote so much about children; they are precious but not in a sentimental way. Children are the clearest image of the beauty of creation.

It's a rare person who sees the mates as beautiful. These retarded people are sisters and brothers, sons and daughters, aunts and uncles, sometimes mothers and fathers and I see their relatives visiting with them. Frustration, love, shame, and embarrassment are skipping around with one another. It's hard to be with an adult who is not an adult. That's not the way it's supposed to be. Something has gone wrong. The relatives of the mates know, I think, that each person who lives here is a good deal more than something that has gone wrong. I write this honestly because some of our people seem to become a single, overbearing function. There are (among others) Jeannette the Smoker, Screaming Bill, Joseph the Weatherman, Alice the Pork Chop—"Are we going to have pork chops today? I like pork chops so much." Alice can say that fifty times a day; each time it seems a new thought. The person becomes a mania. Even in those cases there remains the core of the child who points at something with wonder and won't stop pointing. The mates are people who have not stopped pointing. The pointing has become who they seemingly are.

What we typically do with such people is humor them and try to remember that a human being is in there. We tend to forget that a human being is inside of so-called normal people, too. Everyone is busy being on good or bad behavior. When the relatives come and visit, I get to see both sides of the equation. They are mindful of the person before them who has little to no attention span or who repeats the same thing over and over or who whistles or moans or gulps. They are mindful of themselves, too. They have whistled and moaned and gulped. They have asked the same question when they were anxious or distracted. They have forgotten who was in front of them and what that person was saying. They didn't, however, fall into this gulf. They peer down at the person and their voices take on the oddest inflections—somewhere between coaxing a pet and making an impossible promise. It's heartbreaking but I know that the mates do not suffer from broken hearts. They are too strangely happy.

Innocence is a fearful thing. In America we have turned it into one more aspect of money. You can go to Disneyland and be innocent. What it took to make the money to get you there is another story and one that Americans put aside. When I first started reading Blake, the Songs of Experience were much easier for me than the Songs of Innocence. I knew something about suffering. I was raised in a series of foster homes; some of them were impossible places. I've been attacked and I've fought back. I've lain in bed behind a locked door and watched the handle tremble and shake as someone tries to get in. I've run out into the night and not known where I was going, so I could get away from where I was. I knew about "Marks of weakness, marks of woe," as Blake called it in what to me is the greatest poem of all time, "London." I would never take the word "marks" lightly. If I showed you my arms, you would see what I mean. Part of my sadness is that I fear being touched. I must trust the person's fingers but I don't have much to go by in the way of trust. It's almost impossible for me though I did write "almost." I want to be human. I want to be a person who knows the touch of love.

When I started to read the Songs of Innocence, to let them seep inside me, I cried and cried. "Joy laugh not! Sorrows weep not!" Blake wrote. To feel some of the joy, I have had to go through the sorrow. The sorrow isn't all sad, however, nor is the joy sheer happiness. Everything partakes of the other, "the contrary states of the human soul." Everything that is real daunts words. Joy makes me cry because I can't bear how sweet it is. Sometimes when children become angry, they do something like crossing out a drawing they have done. They hate what they have created. I understand that. Our pain cannot bear the joy that is there in feeling a breeze on our skin or taking a deep breath. Our pain cannot bear the joy that cares not a whit for our troubles. How galling that is. Yet it seems just and right. "Joys impregnate. Sorrows bring forth."

I know most of the lyrics by heart but I still delight in reading them. I imagine that it is like visiting an old friend, one who does not change, who is always there for you. I write "old friend" but I know what I mean is "parent." "The Echoing Green" is such a poem for me:

The Sun does arise,
And make happy the skies;
The merry bells ring
To welcome the Spring;
The skylark and thrush,

The birds of the bush,
Sing louder around
To the bells' cheerful sound,
While our sports shall be seen
On the Echoing Green.

Old John, with white hair,
Does laugh away care,
Sitting under the oak,
Among the old folk.
They laugh at our play,
And soon they all say:
"Such, such were the joys
When we all, girls & boys,
In our youth time were seen
On the Echoing Green."

Till the little one, weary,
No more can be merry;
The sun does descend,
And our sports have an end.
Round the laps of their mothers
Many sisters and brothers,
Like birds in their nest,
Are ready for rest,
And sport no more seen
On the darkening Green.

It's simple, isn't it? But it's not simple. For there to be joy, there must be death. Death is our depth; innocence cannot abolish it. It's good to be alive in this green world. That everything must change is nothing to rue. In that sense, nothing more need be said. Yet we have the likes of poetry to say more, to balance one more alphabet block on top of another alphabet block without making them all topple over. I once took a night school class where some nervous man talked the poems we were reading into a pulp. He thought he was helping us and helping the poems but the poems can take care of themselves. Blake's already have lasted for centuries.

My childhood kept moving in and out of sunlight and shadow as I was shunted from house to house. There were people who wanted me but couldn't keep me because they had too many children already or they had too many troubles already or they got tired. There were people who were evil to me and who smiled crookedly when the social worker came and asked after me. There was a woman who burned me and told me if I said anything I wouldn't live to say more about it. That's when I ran away. I don't write these things to make you feel sorry for me. I don't believe much in feeling sorry. When one of the mates shouts, "Bingo!" the voice is pure joy. It's usually a guttural, uncontrollable throb of pleasure tinged with a fraction of disbelief. Who could believe that from this empty card, bingo should emerge? Sometimes the inspectors stand in the door and shake their intelligent heads. I can feel them thinking, "Harmless fun for harmless people." Indeed.

As activities director at the Minor, Doreen is in charge of the bingo games. A big, florid woman with bad teeth but a quick smile, she knows how enticing bingo is, how there is no tiring of wondering what number comes next. We have games most afternoons. The mates gather in the day room. They come in all sizes and make all sorts of sounds. Some of them look dented and misshapen; their pain is physically manifest. Others seem untouched; their pain is a deep, thin thread wound through their souls. By mid-afternoon we are in what Doreen calls the "med lull." By four-thirty various behaviors will start to announce themselves. The chemical answers will have worn off; the side effects will have arrived. But in the mid-afternoon we are in a modest, fragile trough where people can gather around a common cause—bingo. Some afternoons I find myself ravished by the simple fact of numbers, the harmony that gives us arithmetic. That harmony is mirrored in the sunlight that pours through the west windows and the studious looks the bingo cards are given and the dust motes drifting through the peaceful air.

Then someone stammers or jabbers or whines and I am back to my job. There is no progress in my line of work. We are in the dumb realm of vegetable life. I don't write that to disparage; all humans are in that realm but we push it aside. Swallowing and shitting aren't who we truly are. At the Minor they are. Each day I ponder the geography of bodies as I help to dress them and roll them over and put lotions and salves on them and clean the most private places. The mates are mostly doughy. They love white flour; they don't exercise unless forced. They have no notions of how their bodies should be nor how they should feel. They are lost in wallows of fat. The music of their flesh is a deep, soft groan. Blake loved to draw the musculature of the body. It was palpable energy; his heroes look like Muscle Beach weightlifters. The Minor's inhabitants have lost their bodies to their minds. When someone becomes violent, it's like watching a train careen down a hill. You can sense the engineer of the overmatched train sitting there at the controls and wondering what to do. Twice, people who were afraid of their shadow have given me black eyes.

Most people I've known outside the Minor act as though there is a sensible norm. The body needs the mind and provides for it. The mind is cautious and enjoys itself according to its wiles. All is well. But it isn't. Sometimes I sing Blake's poems to myself in a low voice when I am tending a mate's needs. It can be slow work going over a couple hundred pounds of confused flesh. I sing "The Fly," for instance:

Little Fly,
The summer's play
My thoughtless hand
Has brushed away.

Am not I
A fly like thee?
Or art not thou

A man like me?

For I dance,
And drink, & sing,
Till some blind hand
Shall brush my wing.

If thought is life
And strength & breath,
And the want
Of thought is death;

Then am I
A happy fly,
If I live
Or if I die.

Sometimes when the mates ask me what I am humming, I pick up my voice and sing it more distinctly. They look pleased. It isn't their understanding, of course, that matters. It's their being touched by the lilt of the words, the melody of the meaning. As I help to raise their arms or steady a tottering step, I feel the blind hand that has struck them. I feel the blind hand that has struck me.

We contrive a million stories to make the blind hand go away. I suppose it does for most people, though not for me. I was given the gift of emptiness, of abandonment. A government agency paid for the care I received. As a child I knew that. "Your check has come," my "mother" would say. Sometimes she would look at me wistfully but more often she would look at me with cold anger as if I was the cause of my trouble. To such eyes I was a little figure, a calculation. As was the case with many of the children about whom Blake wrote, I was lost and had no idea of how to be found. I tried to make myself small. No one ever read me a poem. I heard some of the Bible. It told me more things to be afraid of.

You fall into the well of no-self and you think you'll never come out. I know nothing of my parents. I was left under a bench late one night in a Greyhound bus station. I lay there for who knows how long until a janitor came along, noticed a parcel and picked it up. Such things don't happen, we tell ourselves. People don't leave a baby but the people who I assume were my parents did. When I seek their faces in my heart, I get very afraid. It is a place I should not go to but I have to go there and I do. I try to see their faces as they put me down. I try to imagine if they looked back. I try to imagine their steps and the close of a door. I try to imagine myself, the sleeping, swaddled infant. I walk around my apartment when I do this and the cats can feel my hurt. They try to cozy up to me; they know. They hear my voice as I chant the words of "A Little Boy Lost" and "A Little Girl Lost." How could the poet know so much? How could he see so far into the human heart? How is it that we dare to ignore poetry? The words don't still my pain but they tell my pain that it has company. They tell it not to apologize. Sometimes I walk up and down and say a line over and over—"Parents were afar. Parents were afar. Parents were afar." I sound like one of the obsessive mates. The cats bear with me, though. They know what I am feeling; they are fellow creatures. People who think animals don't have feelings are blockheads.

The word "lost" has a terrible ring to me. "Who are your parents?" I was asked when I was growing up. Sometimes it was a well-intentioned question; sometimes it wasn't. What could I reply? Monsters who abandoned me? Confused, desperate people? People who never cared in the first place? People who were on the run? But not murderers. Imagine a child saying that—"My parents were not murderers." They didn't smother me or drop me from a window or batter me. They left me behind. They gave me up to whatever might happen to me. When I answered the question about parents, I insisted that they were away visiting or that they were explorers. I can remember squeezing myself when I said this, putting my arms around myself, hugging myself. As a grown person, poetry helps me stay in my skin:

"Nought loves another as itself,

Nor venerates another so,
Nor is it possible to Thought
A greater than itself to know:

"And Father, how can I love you
Or any of my brothers more?
I love you like the little bird
That picks up crumbs around the door."

I love the mates like that "little bird." I imagine something like an English sparrow, a common bird we don't think twice about, a bird you see each day rummaging through urban litter, happy to share the city with us careless humans. That's what the mates are like; they are happy to share with the world, even though the world mocks them. Sometimes I think of the ridicule each of them has endured, the taunts and ugly remarks, even hatred for their being different. One thing I admire about Blake's God is that he has no use for human judgments. He scorns them. Blake's God is the Great Imaginer, the god who acknowledges "the pride of the peacock," "the lust of the goat," "the wrath of the lion," and "the nakedness of woman." Blake's God acknowledges the mates—not as freaks or imperfections, but as the dire beauties they are. Infinite, pure energy has to exist for there to be finite, impure energy. For there to be "the little bird" and Betty MacLeod, a Minor resident whose only question is whether today is her birthday, there must be more imagination than humans can ever conceive.

I can feel how few souls love Blake's "little bird" when I go out in the world with the mates. Their favorite places are the world's favorite places—McDonald's and Wal-Mart are at the head of the list. I go with Doreen and another aide and we take two mates apiece. We can fit in the big van that has Hill and Dale Manor written on the side along with a castle-like building on top of a hill that looks more like a gopher pile if you ask me. The building I work in is an old, three-story wooden house that must have been a swell place a long time ago but now has been added onto and added onto until it seems as though there are more hallways and stairs than rooms. It's not a castle.

We plan carefully when we take the mates out, what Doreen calls "pre-invasion." We talk with them about where we are going. "I know about Wal-Mart, Doreen. Everyone knows about Wal-Mart. We are going to Wal-Mart." That's Mary Boudreau who responds very well but has a hard time initiating a sentence on her own. Doreen calls her "The Human Echo." Doreen gets a little weary. She wanted to be a cruise ship director and here she is with the ship of fools. She calls me "The Poet," as in "I'd like The Poet to keep an eye on The Echo."

It takes some time to get everyone in the van because there's some bickering about how Human Echo doesn't want to sit next to Screaming Bob and how Joseph the Weatherman has to sit by a window so he can see the sky and how Jeannette stinks from cigarettes and no one wants to be near her. It's like a school bus full of kids except these people are all over fifty. Once we get settled, it's quiet for a while. Everyone is tired from trying to get the right seat. Then everyone is talking all at once about whatever is out there—a kind of car no one has seen before, a new restaurant ("What's Cantonese mean, Doreen? What's Cantonese mean, Doreen?" Questions tend to get repeated at least twice.), pedestrians ("That man looks mean." "That woman looks sweet." "That little girl should be wearing a hat."), police ("Look out for the fuzz!"). When it comes to chatter, the mates are nonpareil.

Before we disembark, we go over behavior expectations. I'm aware at these moments that we are using words and that we need something more than words. We give each hand a squeeze as the person exits the van. I can see the anxiety in their pleading eyes. People they don't know make them nervous. I can't say that I blame them. When people give us the hairy eyeball and a wide berth or make clucking sounds to show they pity us, I recall they are the same people who pitied "poor" William Blake and said he was a lunatic. If people have a chance to get it wrong so that they can feel right, they'll do it every time. If they could burn retarded people in a holy place they would.

The mates all have a purchase to make; no one is here just to gawk.

They are doing their part to keep the wheels of commerce turning. When I walk into a place like Wal-Mart, I ask the William Blake question, which is "What would William Blake think of this?" It's hard to imagine someone who lived just when the machine was overtaking the hand visiting a place so crammed with manufactures. Blake treasured what God created, not what people invented. He treasured originality, not sameness. He treasured the freedom of the senses not the drudgery of desire. Why would we want sameness? It's hard to imagine Blake pushing a cart around and murmuring about bargains and whether he needed to stockpile more oil filters or paper towels. "Enough! or Too Much," he wrote. America might be renamed "Too Much Land." Blake saw the material happiness that was coming; he saw the price we would pay for that happiness.

I get Screaming Bob and Jeannette. Jeannette wants a blue cigarette lighter where "you can see the stuff inside." She already has a number of them but she's a collector. Screaming Bob wants pipe cleaners. He doesn't smoke. He wants to make animals out of pipe cleaners the way Doreen showed the mates a month or so ago. He wants to make horses. He keeps saying "horses" over and over. It might drive some people to drink but I think it's cute. I even like Bob's scaly hand in mine.

These stores are so big you feel as if you're shopping in a county in Texas. When you ask one of the lady salespeople for help, she looks back at you dully as if to say, "Do you think I know anything about this place?" We find an aisle that has cheap accessories and Jeannette finds her lighter. I think the only thing Jeannette really likes is smoking; once she has the lighter she wants to go outside and smoke a cigarette. "Smoke break," she starts saying to me. She likes the sound of it. The mates like the sounds that words make. I used to think they could be poets but then I decided they already were poets. There are just many missing lines.

I tell Jeannette we'll go in a minute. I know she will wait for a minute and start in again. I should have said "three minutes." I tell her to help us look for pipe cleaners. Imagine a store with all the crap Wal-Mart has in it and we are looking for pipe cleaners. Screaming Bob is getting nervous. I can see his face welling up with anguish. He wants his pipe cleaners. Jeannette leers at him as if to say, "I got what I wanted and you are too stupid to get what you want and you deserve it." That doesn't make Bob feel better. He tries to glare back at her but he doesn't have a glare in him.

I can't figure out where the pipe cleaners are and I can't find someone to help and Jeannette starts in again that she needs to smoke and that she needs to use her new lighter and she can't wait. I grab Bob's hand to signal that it's okay; we will find his pipe cleaners so he can make horses but I grip it a little too hard. He starts making the sound that is Bob's scream. It comes from way down inside and begins slowly as if he were fiddling with a radio and trying to get the bass and treble right. That's only for a few seconds, however, and then he's right into it, the agonized wobble of his fraught little-boy's-voice-in-a-grown-man's-voice. He's a living siren. He's a nightmare howl that won't quit. He's chaos. His eyes close tightly and his face is scrunched up. He doesn't know where he is; he only knows that he needs to scream.

I don't freak out. I feel kind of happy: not that Bob is upset but that he is letting his feelings rip. He's not about to court that prudence Blake described as a "rich, ugly old maid." Jeannette looks at me and waits for me to start soothing Bob, a process that can take quite a while. He won't hear anything for a couple of minutes. He's gone. All I can do is hold his hand so he doesn't take off because he's swaying back and forth like an old Jewish man at his prayers or an out-of-whack metronome. He can run seriously amok at this moment.

Since I know I can't do much beyond hold his hand and since Wal-Mart bugs me more than I can say with all the sad merchandise people are spending their lives handling and eyeing and scheming to get and then buying and forgetting, I start screaming, too. It's a little scream compared to Bob's but it's a healthy scream, it's got some decibels. Jeannette looks at me startled-like. I can see she wants to report me to Doreen because she's that sort of person, a tattletale, but then her eyes get funny as if she were experiencing indigestion and she starts screaming, too. It's a happy, girlish scream, though; you'd think she just won the Miss America pageant.

I feel something rising out of me as I scream. It isn't my orphanhood but it's something close to it, my feeling that I don't know where I am in this world because I don't know where I came from. I feel I do know where I am—I'm in Wal-Mart screaming with two retarded people. "No bird soars too high, if he soars with his own wings," Blake wrote. I feel that I'm weirdly soaring, that my soul is gliding on a thermal of harsh sound. I came into this world as innocent as any child but harshness attended me and brought me low. I have the right to scream. Bob has the right to scream. Jeannette has the right to scream. It's so real, it's beautiful, a throbbing pandemonium. If you don't like it, you can call security.

That doesn't happen because Doreen has heard us and she shows up waving the silver bullet—pipe cleaners. She's shouting the words with titanic glee. "Pipe cleaners! Pipe cleaners!" Shoppers have cleared out of our aisle by this time; Joseph the Weatherman, who is one of Doreen's charges, is staring at us with something like awe but Bob hears the words, and as suddenly as the squall seems to have started, it stops. Bob opens his little eyes, looks at the pipe cleaners, and says what you would expect him to say, which is "pipe cleaners." Jeannette and I have stopped screaming because Bob clearly was the lead vocalist. We, too, stare at the pipe cleaners. Doreen stops shouting. We can hear the sounds of the store once again—shopping carts rattling along, bored kids scuffing their sneakers, the ventilation system wheezing. It feels downright tranquil.

We make our way to the cash registers. Jeannette clutches her lighter; Bob clutches his pipe cleaners so tightly I notice the light cardboard in which they are packaged is crumpling. Both Bob and Jeannette have the look of children who have been given a gift they wanted but did not expect to receive. They are beaming like little suns. If in a few hours, Bob starts swaying and keening and Jeannette is smoking feverishly, this still has been a good trip.

I look around me for any signs of William Blake. I believe his spirit is still on the earth. Wherever air moves, there is spirit, even here in this vast, ugly, cinderblock monstrosity. What I notice right off is an old man who is smiling. He has big, white eyebrows and watery blue eyes. He's short the way

Blake was a short, stocky man. I don't think he is smiling at us. He is inner smiling. He doesn't have anything in his hands, however; so he isn't smiling out of possessiveness. He seems to be waiting for someone. I take it in and have the old feeling—this man could be my father. I'm always looking at people's faces; I can't help it. But when I'm looking at his face, I'm not looking for what will solve the mystery of me. The mystery of me is endless. Some great grief made it; some joy redeemed it.

William Carlos Williams, b.1883

My wife died three years ago of pancreatic cancer. It came on fast. One day she was driving the car to get groceries and visit our daughter and the grandchildren across town; then I was in the hearse on the way to the cemetery. I'm a retired pharmacist so I've been around medicine my whole life. Once we got the diagnosis, I knew that she was a goner. Doctors will offer some hope if there is some hope, but the specialist told Helen she should check her will. We held hands when we left his office, her little hand in my big paw. We walked very slowly to the parking lot. I felt that if I walked slowly maybe I could stall time. "Lots of luck," as my buddy Jimmy Pappas likes to say.

We were married for forty-nine years. Helen was planning a party for our fiftieth. She was outgoing, had lots of girlfriends, and loved to give parties and help other people give parties. She was a planner, always a couple of moves ahead of everyone else, always attending to the details, making lists. Whenever I start talking about her, I don't know where I am. I look around me as if saying her name will make her appear. It's pitiful, but the person you live with becomes like a wristwatch or a light in the hall that never gets turned off. I don't mean those things in a disrespectful way. They're my way of saying that I was used to Helen and loved her. We never wore each other out. She knew when to leave me be; she knew when to get close to me. How did she know that? Was that something female she was born with? It's funny how you have these questions that you could have asked any day for forty-nine years. Now I'm talking to myself and the clock on the living room wall.

When I was running my pharmacy, I was on my feet all day talking to customers, employees, salesmen. I especially liked the customer part, shooting the breeze with people about whatever was on their mind. Nowadays, pharmacists work in huge, cinderblock buildings for some mega-corporation. They're serfs. I can't stand to go into one of those places and look the pharmacist in the eye. Everything in this country gets systematized but that's not to the benefit of the people who are doing the work. That's to the benefit of money making more money. I was a businessman myself, but I don't think you can miss that one. I can't imagine these people standing there under a battery of fluorescent lights and breathing air that has been sitting around since Jimmy Carter was president are having a good time. They aren't handing out peppermints to kids and taking time to talk baseball, I can tell you that. They look like they haven't smiled a real smile in a month; instead, they smile that pinched, I'm-doing-my-best-leave-me-alone smile. Meanwhile, the drug companies are making out like bandits. You hate to see your own profession go down the tubes.

When Helen died, I got tired of talking. People were nervous around me and didn't know what to say. Even the ones who were close to us were nervous. Sometimes they looked somber and asked me if I wanted to talk and paused but I shook my head "no." What I inevitably would talk about would be the past and when you have lost the closest person to you the past becomes a strange place. You feel how words don't add up to much. As a talker, I can't say I ever thought about that. I spewed them out; there were more from where those came from. Like Helen I was outgoing; I didn't lack for a quip. But when Helen died I started to hate words because they were so general: "Well, we got to be with each other for a lot of years. I'm not complaining." Or "We had our ups and downs but we hung in there together." Or "When I look back there I see Helen's face smiling at me." You get my drift. You're always summarizing because no one wants to listen to the details. People are willing to listen some but not too much. They want an idea of what something was like that they can nod their heads to. But I didn't live with Helen in an idea. We raised three children together, for starters. That's no idea. When your son has fallen off his bicycle and his leg looks like it's on the wrong way, that's not an idea.

In the words of my daughter Kim, the one who lives across town (my other two kids live downstate), I was someone who "became withdrawn." I didn't think of myself that way. I kept busy the way you keep busy when you're suddenly on your own. I made sure the house was tidy, the way Helen would have liked it. I looked after my investments. Beginning with the sports pages I read the local paper every day. I went for walks and visited with old friends and played cribbage. I went over to Kim's a couple of times a week and spent time with my grandchildren or helped her husband Ryan work on the addition they were putting onto their house. I'm good with my hands and love to build anything. One year I made enough bird houses for the whole damn town. Still, I stayed away from groups—bereavement groups, senior citizen groups, church groups. If you ask me, this country is group crazy. Everybody has to be in a group or they're considered some weirdo who's going to shoot up the local supermarket. I don't know what's with all these groups. Are we that lonely?

I speak as someone who has come to know what silence is. I wake up in the middle of the night and for a second or two I think I'm going to look over and Helen will be there. It's like what they call a phantom limb where you lose a leg or an arm and still have the feeling that it's there. I wake up and then there's the moment when I realize that I'm a big dope and she's dead. I don't mind admitting that I've cried at some of those moments. Why shouldn't I cry? There I am in our bed and she's not there. It's our bed. It's a bed a men and a woman slept in for decades and felt each other's body in the most intimate ways you can feel another body. Now all that's there when I wake up is nothing. Sometimes I say her name to get rid of the silence, but that makes it worse. I take a piss or get myself a little ginger ale from the refrigerator. Then I lie down again with the silence. It makes me feel empty inside. I've never felt like that.

I could let the TV become my companion, but I don't want to do that. I know people who do that; they talk about the television as if it were another person. I have to say that to me that is sick. I understand why they do it. Human beings want the presence of other human beings who are busy doing whatever they are doing—talking politics or shooting bad guys or falling in love or telling jokes or living on desert islands. But the presence of human beings on a screen isn't the same thing as another living human being. It's what is called a "simulacrum." (I've been doing word puzzles forever and I know some words.) As my father, who was a jeweler, liked to say, "It's glass. It's not the real thing." It became an expression around our house when I was growing up—"It's glass." Well, let me tell you, TV is glass. Maybe, that's why it's so popular. It doesn't have to be anything. It can be as stupid as it wants and no one cares. In fact, it's better if it's stupid because you don't have to think twice about what you are doing watching it. You can enjoy the stupidity or you can make fun of it: "I'm smarter than this stuff." You may be smarter, but if you spend a lot of time watching it, you are as glass as it is. I don't want that to happen to me.

You might think that my going for walks doesn't mean much, that I'm another geriatric case who's out there to keep the blood circulating, but there's more to it than exercise. I grew up in this town and I'll die here. I'm not going to Florida and sit around with the other old birds and talk about how glad I am that I never have to look at a snowflake again. To hell with that—the state of Florida is a big outdoor mortuary. Here, I know where I am and who I am. It's not that it's beautiful. They don't call it the Rustbelt for nothing. Still, it's what I know. Kim tells me to watch where I go, but it's daylight and no one has done anything yet. I was a pharmacist. I know what dope is and I know what's happening on some of those streets. I could tell you stories till the middle of next week about what people do to themselves with pills. Sometimes, though I knew how much they were hurting, I had to cut people off. A mountain of bad scrip got pushed across my counter. Twice guys came in with guns. I gave them what they wanted and called the cops when they left. Both times I looked in their faces (they didn't have masks on) and could see, even though I was frightened by the guns, how messed up they were. I felt worse for them than I did for myself. If hell has a face that's what they looked like.

I take my daily walks and along the way I pick up whatever little things I need. My daughter Kimmie (that's what Helen and I always called her) started referring to me as the Ancient Gofer. She asked me if I wanted a dog to keep me company. I told her I've had enough dog shit for one lifetime. She also kept at me about needing to do more with myself than walk. I told her "no groups," but you never stop humoring your children. That's what brought me to sign up for a class in medicine and literature at the local college. They've got special classes for old people and I qualify on that count. Plenty of days when I get back from my walk, I need a good long nap.

That's how I came to learn about William Carlos Williams. It's not as though I don't read books. I read a lot, though I tend to read my favorite writers over and over again—Mark Twain, for instance. I've read *Huckleberry Finn* three or four times. He's funny and he's smart, Mark Twain. He knew that how people acted and how they said they acted were different planets. He must have gotten angry at times but he had the grace to be humorous. Poetry, however, was something else. I read some poems in high school but that's it. Since that must have been gents like Henry Wadsworth Longfellow and John Greenleaf Whittier (with names like that you know they weren't Greek immigrants), I can say that I probably never read anything by a twentieth-century American poet. I knew who Robert Frost was from pictures in *Life* magazine that I used to look at when I was getting my hair cut. He had a pleased look that showed he was enjoying being famous. Everyone knows what a big deal it was when he got to read a poem at JFK's inauguration. I don't recall seeing any pictures of William Carlos Williams in *Life*, however. In fact, I never heard of the guy. Maybe there was only room for one famous poet in the United States, though given how big this country is that doesn't make much sense.

The class is kind of Mickey Mouse. The young profs who teach it (one's in literature and the other's in medicine) figure we're old and our brains are turning to mush so they better not push us too hard. They also figure knowledge should be entertaining. They tell us lots of stories about the writers and they tell us about research that shows literature can help people feel better. That didn't exactly seem like a revelation but I kept my mouth shut. Sitting on an uncomfortable, molded plastic chair, I found myself getting impatient with the whole thing. It wasn't as though I had never opened a book before or hadn't thought about how a good one could boost a person's spirits. One morning, however, about four weeks into the course (which only ran seven weeks anyway on account of our mushy brains), the literature professor handed out a poem by William Carlos Williams.

When you are used to reading novels like *Huckleberry Finn* a poem doesn't look very impressive. A novel or a biography or a history book is like an automobile from the 1950s—big and wide—but a poem is a Volkswagen Beetle. I could never see myself driving around in something that looked like a tin can on wheels. It seemed as though if you burped the thing would explode. When I looked at the poem for the first time I can't say that I was excited. Plus the literature prof, who is a good, well-meaning kid in his thirties, tends to drone when he reads. I don't know where he's been, but I get the feeling he's never raised his voice in his life.

Williams, I learned, was a doctor who traveled around doing house calls and was prone to writing poems whenever he had a minute to grab. I liked that he was a doc who was out in the world and knew something about people. My notion of a poet was of someone who sits on his or her ass, stares out a window, and has someone around who brings in the drinks and meals. I thought of poets as people who live on a higher plane of existence than the rest of us and have pulled the ladder up after them. I thought of poetry as too good for the rest of us. But Williams wrote poems and he was still a doctor down in Jersey. Everyone knows what Jersey is like; it's not a higher plane of anything.

The poem the prof read to us and that he handed out to us as a photocopy was from a book called *Spring and All*. He said that it's the first poem in the book:

> By the road to the contagious hospital
> under the surge of the blue
> mottled clouds driven from the
> northeast—a cold wind. Beyond, the
> waste of broad, muddy fields
> brown with dried weeds, standing and fallen
>
> patches of standing water
> the scattering of tall trees
>
> All along the road the reddish

purplish, forked, upstanding, twiggy
stuff of bushes and small trees
with dead, brown leaves under them
leafless vines—

Lifeless in appearance, sluggish
dazed spring approaches—

They enter the new world naked,
cold, uncertain of all
save that they enter. All about them
the cold, familiar wind—

Now the grass, tomorrow
the stiff curl of wildcarrot leaf
One by one objects are defined—
It quickens: clarity, outline of leaf

But now the stark dignity of
entrance—Still, the profound change
has come upon them: rooted, they
grip down and begin to awaken

The prof told us that Doctor Williams was keen on trying to "honor the physical world" (I wrote the phrase down), that he believed that ideas resided in things, and that a poet gave you those things in the form of images. As I said, he didn't raise his voice, but you could tell that in his prof way he was excited because he paced around in the front of the room. He said a lot else about Williams, but I wasn't listening. I was staring at the poem, which seemed to me to be in a foreign language. I know that sounds stupid because it's right there in English, plain as day, but no one I could recall ever wrote anything that looked like that poem.

At first, reading the poem made me nervous. I could take it in when the prof read it, about the leaves and the grass and the trees and spring starting to get going. I understood that, but when I looked down at the poem, it seemed another world to me. The lines didn't go all the way to the right-hand side of the page the way they do in prose. I know poems do that, but I have no idea why they do that. And the lines ended in funny places, like with the word "the." Why would he end one of these lines with the word "the"? Is "the" supposed to be a big deal? Or maybe it's not at all a big deal and that's why it's there at the end of the line. The poet wants you to think about how it's a word, too. That got my attention because no one goes around thinking about "the." As far as words are concerned, "the" is lint.

I could go on about this kind of stuff, how there are no periods to speak of and how he has dashes all over the place. Actually, that's what I do when I have to write something like a note to someone. Writing notes was Helen's province, but every now and then I had to thank someone in writing for something and I wound up with not many periods and a lot of dashes. Did that make me a poet? I don't think so. Still, when I thought about it while the prof kept talking, I could imagine that Doctor Williams had his reasons. It made me feel sort of jiggly when I was reading the poem, as though the things in the poem were going to take off any minute. They didn't take off, but you felt that they could. It seemed almost dramatic, these leaves trying to come out into the cold world.

I started to feel, when I was driving home, that it wasn't a foreign language. It was a different language but not a foreign one. It was a language that considered each word very carefully. As an amateur woodworker who understands the care that has to go into making something, to say nothing of spending decades very deliberately measuring fluids and dosages and powders, I could appreciate that. There were no words that didn't matter; he was practicing an economy—no wasted motion. When I got home, I sat down in my Barca-lounger in the living room and studied the poem. I hadn't studied anything in a long time. It was peaceful, my sitting there with this poem. Since Helen died, I haven't felt much in the way of peace.

I'm not sure how long I did that. Maybe an hour, maybe more. Maybe I dozed off a bit. What surprised me was that the more time I spent with the poem, the more interested in the poem I became. I wondered about how he did it, how he was able to use these words and make this poem out of all the possible poems that could get written. I also started thinking about what he was writing about. I have to say that interested me the most, because what he was writing about was not a big deal. He wasn't writing about his wife of forty-nine years dying of some miserable cancer. He wasn't writing about her husband living on in their house and wondering why he still was alive. He was writing about how spring starts to come. I could appreciate that, because when you live upstate, spring is a long time in coming. You're impressed and surprised that it comes at all. Sometimes, you think the plants and trees and shrubs must have forgotten what warm weather is like. It's still cold when spring begins up here. I noticed that he used that word "cold" three times in the poem. He's not letting you forget it, about how winter doesn't want to let go.

I liked, too, how he described things. Nothing is beautiful and jumping up and down and saying, "Hey, I'm special, look at me." It's more like what I see on my walks, a lot of stuff that is brown, a lot of stuff that looks like it got run over, a lot of stuff like burdock and thistle that has grown up helter-skelter and is what it is, which is pretty homely. Some days it's hard to tell the trash from the foliage. Our town was an industrial hub once, locomotives were built here, but that was a long time ago. Now there are a lot of empty brick buildings with sumacs and poplars growing by them, trees you don't go and buy in a nursery to plant in your backyard. They're trying to grow, though; even the wild carrot is trying. I know what wild carrot looks like and Doctor Williams described it very well when he wrote "stiff curl." He nailed it.

It's not just things, though, that he writes about. Take, for instance, the word "dignity" in the last stanza of the poem. It's a word no one uses much any more because there's not much dignity left in this country. I'm not a radical, but you look at the Bozo who's the president and he's got as much dignity as my grandsons jumping up and down in their wading pool. Smiling a big smile and telling people that everything is okay is not the same thing as dignity. Dignity is like my brother Johnny who came back from World War II with shrapnel in him that they couldn't operate on and that hurt him every day of the years he had left. He didn't complain. He didn't make a fuss. He didn't ask for pity or charity. He conducted himself with dignity. I know that some leaves on a tree aren't a person, but I can see they have their dignity, too. Doctor Williams makes me feel that.

I kept going back and looking at the poem. Like a song or like one of Helen's layer cakes that she would leave under a big Tupperware dome on the kitchen table, it kept drawing me back. I thought I had the poem pinned down in my head, but I started to realize that I didn't. So I had to keep going back, which was okay because I felt that I was learning a new way of thinking. That sounds a little crazy, "a new way of thinking." It's not something I would say to the guys I play cribbage with. But I think it's true. What I started to feel was that there was a connection between language, which after all I've been using for a long time, and walking around and seeing what's happening around me. Although it's about words, it's hard to put into words what I'm talking about. It's a feeling that the world makes more sense than you ever suspected—much more sense. The problem is that you don't have the words to get there, or I should say that you don't have the careful words because the words have got to be careful. Because they are careful doesn't mean they are dull. It means that the words have a precision to them. The contagious hospital poem has those words.

That's a lot to feel about a piece of writing that's not about something on the evening news. Most of life, though, doesn't make the evening news. We're just walking around from day to day and being busy in our heads with whatever is going on up there. I know that because I lie in bed at night and argue with my past. I should have gotten out of my store five years earlier but I was stubborn and hung on, though the property values kept sinking. Or I should have traveled more with Helen. She wanted to travel, but all I wanted to do was go to our place on the lake, fish, and drink a beer. ""It's pretty here," she would say to me, "but it's isn't Buckingham Palace or the Vatican."

I blew her off the way that men blow women off. Or I could have spent more time with my brother Johnny when he was starting to fail. He never would have asked me to help him out specially or spend extra time with him. I knew, though, what was happening. I was selfish. I was a chump.

Thinking about these things turns me over and over. I get mad at myself. Sometimes when I'm lying there in our bed, I talk out loud and even start yelling. It's as though I'm in a courtroom and the judge is pronouncing a sentence and I start yelling at the judge about how I'm sorry and to give me another chance. I know that yelling at the darkness isn't a good sign of anything. My past feels like a smokescreen. Sometimes it feels as if I'm choking on it. I can feel the smoke right down to my lungs. It stings.

Somehow, that little poem by William Carlos Williams penetrates the smokescreen. It's not explicitly about feelings. He doesn't come out and start singing like in an opera, but feelings are there. That moves me. That seems like a mystery to me. I'm a scientific type who never uses the word "mystery." Someone doesn't come into your pharmacy and ask for two hundred milligrams of mystery. And the poem certainly doesn't seem like a mystery. He sees these things by the roadside. It's a cold day. There's a landscape around him. He writes about it. That's it. It's almost like some kind of code, how the lines fit together, except that it isn't a code.

Whatever it is, I'm grateful that I came across it because during the next week I kept looking at that one poem. You'd think I'd become a professor. I have favorite lines—for instance, "They enter the new world naked...." I like that very much, how decisive that is yet gentle. My whole life's been spent in the English language but I don't think I ever said that I liked a certain word. Our children's names—Kim, Michael and Barbara—I liked those, but those are special; they're names. The words in the poem are un-special words that he makes special. I went to the library and took out a book by him, a whole book of poems.

When I go for walks now, I find myself thinking about how a poet might think. I'm not writing down poems of my own. Maybe I will eventually, maybe I won't. What interests me is the manner of thinking. When I take a more or less typical walk from my house to downtown and then over to the park and then back home, which is over three miles, I look differently at what's around me. It starts when I turn around and look at our house. I know I will call it "our house" until I leave this world because it was our house, Helen's and mine. It's brick, two floors, three bedrooms (the girls slept in the same room when they were growing up), has a side porch with awnings on it. The front steps are concrete. Michael used to play step ball on them with one of those little rubber balls they call a "pinkie." What I wonder is how a poet like Doctor Williams would see the house, what he would write about it. I imagine he's driving down the street in the old days when doctors made house calls. He goes by this house and it gets into his head, this particular house. Maybe he notices something like a couple of the uprights in the porch railing are loose or how rain that has flowed out of the downspout has made a bald spot on the ground.

I know he wouldn't describe it the way I just did. That's not poetry. I know enough to know that. One thing you notice when you read the contagious hospital poem is that it isn't simply a description of a bunch of things. It's more about a process, about what's happening when late winter becomes spring. It's not a process the way something is automatic. It's flukier, more day to day and moment to moment. It's not something that gets onto the TV; it doesn't even get onto the weather report. It's more like what's happening on the earth with living things. What I think, though, and I have a suspicion Doctor Williams would agree with me, is that everything on earth is a living thing one way or another. The bricks that our house is built of are living, too. They don't seem to change much from day to day to the human eye, but I know they change because I've lived in the house long enough to see them lose some of their deep orange-red color and become more of a brown orange-red. It's probably pollution that is doing that. We get plenty of it blowing over from Ohio and Michigan and we also make our own. Still, it's something that's happening. That's what I'm trying to get at. When I read the library book of Doctor Williams's poems, I can see that something is always happening in each poem because something is always happening in the world we live in.

It's that simple. What I'd guess Doctor Williams caught on to is that he didn't have to have a big topic like the three-name poets I read in high school. "Brown leaves" were good enough.

I can't say that knowing this has made me any happier. It doesn't bring my wife back, but it does change how I look at things. When I go for a walk, I don't only look for which storefronts have changed. It's not that I was blind before. I spent my life as a pharmacist and I noticed things most people wouldn't think twice about. People walked in with some serious problems; you could see it in little confusions, how a button wasn't buttoned or a hat was askew. You could hear it in people's voices, how they spoke too fast or too slow. So I'm alert, but I can't say I've been alert in the way the contagious hospital poem is alert. I can't say I ever did that kind of thinking and feeling at the same time. I noticed yesterday, for instance, how a store window was cleaned unevenly and how there was a thin streak of dirt across the top of it. Or I noticed how a woman who was stopped in her car at a traffic light put on pink lipstick while she was waiting for the light to change. Or I noticed how the wind blew an empty paper cup on the sidewalk almost upright. I probably noticed these things before, but I feel that now that they are closer to me. "That could be in a poem" is what I think to myself. I don't want to flood the world with poems, but it could be. I get a kick out of that.

Being by myself, I think a lot about what I am doing still being here when the person who meant the most to me in this world is dead. I know I have three children and I have grandchildren, but that's not the same thing. When you live with another person for a long time, they become your own vitality. They become your sense of what living is all about. You ask them a thousand questions and you give them a thousand answers to their questions. You think, even as you get older and you see that the other person is getting older, too, that somehow your life together is going to go on forever. I know, of course, that it doesn't. When you watch someone's death rattle, you know that time breaks like everything else.

As a human being I'm back on my own, "naked" as Doctor Williams would put it. I know that Helen would want me to keep living. I think, though, that part of me forgot what that was—being on my own. Being alive becomes automatic. We take in what we need to and leave the rest at the door. It's not so much that we stop having our own thoughts as much as we stop having our own feelings. What I'm finding, as I read through his book, is that Doctor Williams didn't leave much at the door. He saw that if you give it a chance, everything speaks to your feelings. It makes me sad that I can't share what I've learned with my wife. She would have been amused at my taking to poetry, but I think she would have been touched, too. Women know that men have things inside of them that men themselves don't know about.

I still wake up in the middle of the night and lie there. I don't turn on the television. What I do is pick up the book of Doctor Williams's poems. Maybe I'll turn to other poets, but right now he is all I need to know about poetry. I read a poem or two and let the poem sort of settle inside of me. I don't worry about it. I don't think about how much I like it or whether I like another one better. I lie there and let the words rattle around. When I turn off the light, I don't usually fall right back asleep. The past is still there for me and I can feel it. I can feel Helen's presence in the house. It's not creepy, though. I sometimes say a few words of a poem to myself, often from the contagious hospital poem because that was the first one and it's become precious to me—"sluggish / dazed spring approaches...." I lie there and I can sense that death is shifting around in my bones and will make its presence known one of these days. What if I had never known that poetry like Doctor Williams's existed? What if I hadn't been given this gift? I don't ask myself why it had to happen now, toward the end of my life. I'm trying to accept it. I'm gripping down.

Elinor Wylie, b. 1885

Mrs. Mansfield, who teaches Junior Year English, likes to have us do reports on writers. She talks about "the writers" as though they were a bunch of aunts and uncles who were coming to the shore for summer vacation. "You should hear what Jane Austen said about George Eliot. Have you seen what Ernie Hemingway looks like? He's been hitting the bottle, no doubt about it." She's proprietary in that way high school English teachers become proprietary. I guess if you teach The *Old Man and the Sea* for twenty or thirty years, you start to feel as though Ernie is a member of your family. That's a long time to spend with a mystic fish story. I've got enough family as it is, but Mrs. Mansfield only has one kid and she's grown up and lives on the other side of the country where she teaches high school English, too. Mrs. Mansfield says they talk on the phone about their classes and "the writers." I can't imagine talking to my mom about the time of day, but maybe, as everyone is always urging me, I'll understand things better when I'm older.

According to Mrs. Mansfield the reports can help teenagers reach that understanding. We won't be sitting in our hard plastic seats chewing gum and admiring our chartreuse fingernail polish forever. As my dad is too fond of saying, "There's a world out there." He points toward the front of the house when he says that as if there were no world in the back of the house. Mrs. Mansfield is too sincere and decent to use that obnoxious phrase "grow up," which sounds as though what the irritated, out-of-patience adult really means is "drop dead." She has a soft, fluty voice that seems incongruous, because she's squat as a fire hydrant or as Joe Klein, the self-appointed class clown, puts it, "a female fullback." She uses lots of well-meaning words like "share" and "empathy" and "diversity." Sometimes I wish she were a little more sophisticated and little less earnest but look who she's dealing with—a room full of sixteen- and seventeen-year-olds, which means horny, giggly, and volatile while cultivating an aura of cosmic indifference and supernatural awareness. Passing out literature to the likes of us every September would make me wince, but Mrs. Mansfield coos and burbles. She believes in the books. They are her permanent friends.

Mostly we do reports on novelists. They are the number-one guys in the author tribe. They are so big-time that we read some of them in translation and forget that they wrote in another language. After the novelists come the dramatists because of Shakespeare and Arthur Miller. I've read *Death of a Salesman* and *The Crucible* more times (twice) than I've read *Hamlet* (once). Then come the short story writers and the essayists. Then come the poets. They're at the bottom. You don't expect to hear about the poets from some of the English teachers who are more coaches than teachers, like Mr. Notley, who coaches boys' basketball and has diagrams of plays on his blackboard. But even teachers like Mrs. Mansfield who are keen on literature don't seem to want to spend much time with the poets. In April the poets pop up in a unit for a couple of weeks with the daffodils. All year long we slog through the novels and plays and then we hit the poets. It feels funny after reading those big books. (I read the books. Cliff Notes depress me. They're like hearing someone summarize a great party that you weren't invited to.) You read something like *Grapes of Wrath* that goes on forever and puts you through so much and then you're looking at twenty lines of Robert Frost or Emily Dickinson. What happened?

Mrs. Mansfield makes a big fuss about choosing the poets for our reports. We don't really choose because we don't know anything. Most of the names of so-called famous twentieth-century poets are strictly names to the uneducated likes of us. That's why our reports are oral: by listening to one another we get to learn the difference between fancy names like T. S. Eliot and Edna St. Vincent Millay. We pull slips of paper out of a hat. It's corny but it's something different and that's always appreciated. It's an index of how boring high school is that we get excited over a fire drill. How lame is that? You get to stand outside for five minutes and blab with your friends. It could even turn into ten minutes if the principal feels we haven't shown proper fire drill speediness in leaving the building. Wow! How great is that? Ten minutes in the cold talking about how cold you are. It's better, though, than sitting in algebra class. So pulling the names out of a fedora (being an English teacher, Mrs. Mansfield likes to name everything properly) is better than being assigned poets from a list. School irons your soul right out.

I went to the school library and got a book of poems by the name on the slip—Elinor Wylie—and a biography of her. I looked at the lender's cards. Once a year each book had been taken out by a kid who had to do a report on Elinor Wylie. Three years ago it was Katie Maxwell who used to go with my brother John before he fell for Susan Carmichael and dumped Katie. I remember thinking she was pretty cool because she liked Bob Dylan and made no bones about it. Too many kids are namby-pamby about their musical tastes. Susan Carmichael, for instance, used to praise whatever I happened to be listening to—Los Lobos, Joni Mitchell, and Led Zep were all the same to her. She had bigger tits, though. I doubt if my brother's brain goes much further than that. I told him that he should do it right and get involved with a go-go dancer. I won't tell you what he told me to do.

Since I didn't have swim practice until later in the afternoon that day when I got the books, I spent some time checking out the photos of her. I wanted to get a sense of what she looked like before I started reading her poems and about her life. I like looking at pictures of people, actually. It's sort of moony, staring at faces and trying to feel who a person is, but I read somewhere that the face is the window of the soul. My English teacher last year, Mr. Proctor, says that my generation is "visually oriented," which is a polite way of saying "illiterate." Mr. Proctor is gay and a real honey. I used to get the feeling that sometimes in the classroom he was actually thinking, which is an uncommon classroom feeling. It's nothing against Mrs. Mansfield that I wish I had him again. School is like the cafeteria, though. You have to take what they serve when they serve it. Last year a very quiet kid named Andrew Kellogg looked down at a plate of the congealed cardboard they call macaroni and cheese and chucked it across the room with a real quick wrist motion as if it were a Frisbee. It splattered on the wall where they post announcements of fascinating things like the bus schedule and the school nurse's hours. At first, everyone was silent with shock but then people stood up and started cheering: "Way to go, Andy!" and "You the man!" He got suspended for a week. I heard they made him apologize to each of the cafeteria workers individually.

The portraits of Elinor Wylie are in black and white and feel as though they are from longer ago than they really are. Around World War I is a long time ago, but they have that feeling that time lends to how people do their hair and how they dress and just generally look. To me people from the past look lost, as if time had blinded them. Maybe it's because you know they are dead now. It's creepy. Even if you're a kid like me you can't help but realize how your ticket is out there waiting to get punched. Two springs ago a senior who'd been accepted on early admission to Dartmouth and was a big lacrosse player got killed in a car crash. We walked around dazed and tearful and then more days went by and we started to forget.

Elinor Wyle was a pretty woman who knew she was a pretty woman. You can feel she knew that from the determined set of her mouth. She's all business but there's also a feeling of female tenderness. She's pale and her dark hair stands out like a mystery you can touch. There's a smidgen of self-satisfaction, too. She knows she can be the center of the show if she wants to be. She may not want to but it's her choice. That means a lot of stuff is buzzing around in her head. Though she looks composed, the way everyone used to look composed instead of electric and raggedy which is how people look now, she could be confused. Then again, she's pretty and that goes a long way down the field.

She looks demure. That's a word I learned in vocabulary because you never hear someone say that word in day-to-day life. It's definitely not a real- world, high school word. Only women can look demure. I'm not sure about it. In one photo which is clearly from when she was quite young—in her early twenties maybe—she seems barely there. She's looking down and she's set in a cameo. Her dress is white and the area around her person is white, also. Her lips are set in that pensive, delicate way. It's as if she's going to disappear or she's showing you she's there but she could disappear. Or it's as if women are supposed to be sort of there and not there at the same time. Or she's creating herself even though someone is taking a picture of her. As I say, I don't know. It's haunting, though, how perfect she seems because even I know by my feeble age that no one is anywhere near perfect.

Maybe a lot of women looked like Elinor. If you walk down the halls of my high school, you might start thinking you are seeing the same girl over and over. She's got on lip-gloss and tight jeans and shoes with heels. She's thin and her hair is on the long side and not permed. It's a natural look but it's carefully tended. It's not like the sixties, let's-be-hippies look. I think we all want to be models but we're not sure what we are modeling. We want to be loved for who we are but we don't know who that is beyond our bodies, which we tend endlessly. I'm no different when it comes to spending time on myself in the bathroom. Sometimes I think I'm happiest when I'm washing my hair. I learned later when I read the biography that Elinor had her own bathroom and didn't let anyone else in. You could say that she was vain but that seems a harsh word. She was shoring herself up as a woman and putting herself out there as a woman. You can't get around it. The girls at school who go with the grunge look—loose shirts and baggy pants—are still girls.

It mattered to me that the poet I had to do my report on was a woman. Being a girl or young woman or even "young lady" (which is what my father calls me when he's about to lecture me) is tricky. Maybe it's tricky because each of those female nouns says something different. Looking at Elinor's portraits that day in the school library, I could sense that she was a lady and that the word meant something to her. How she acted and when she acted mattered a great deal. There were lots of rules that went with being a lady. I wondered what they were because the rules I knew tended to be basic, such as don't chew with your mouth open. When I looked at Elinor, I felt that even at my neatest I was a slob.

She intimidated me. That was a weird feeling because I was never going to meet her. She was just a famous dead person. Still, I could feel a laser-like intensity about her. Sometimes when you look at pictures of long-ago people, you can't imagine them walking out of the picture and into life. I could imagine Elinor walking right into life. I know I would have given her a wide berth but I would have wanted to be her friend, too. She wasn't your typical housewife. I could sense that the eyes that looked coolly down from her photo could burn a hole in you.

I became an expert on Elinor Wylie. Granted that means a high school expert, which means I read two biographies and her collected poems. Still, that's nothing to spit at, as my father would phrase it in his genteel way. For two months I was something like obsessed. That was good because the reports came due during prom time. Actually, they came due during the time when you get asked to the prom. There's an unofficial time in March when guys start asking girls to the prom which is more like official except there aren't any signs up around school about it such as "Been Asked to the Prom Yet?" or "Eat Your Heart Out." Winter sports are over, which means swim team for me; spring sports haven't started and everyone is thinking that good weather is almost here. Your hormones really start hopping in March. The prom itself is exciting because it's fun to dress up but you want to be there with someone you like or at least someone you can stand for an evening. That can be tricky.

I had a crush on Liam Baker. He's tall, smart, has beautiful wavy brown hair and is sweet in that masculine way that guys can be sweet that combines strength with sensitivity and makes me weak in the knees. Half the girls in the school had a crush on Liam who was good-natured about his popularity, not conceited. I actually think he was a little overwhelmed by it. One year he was another guy joking around in the gym lobby where they let us play hacky sack and then he was Prince Charming. I wanted to get my hands on him and I wanted him to get his hands on me.

Actually, I wanted to go all the way with him—homerun, touchdown, whatever sports metaphor you prefer. I hadn't done it yet. I'd been through some moments that featured some very heavy breathing—hands on my chest, hands in my panties, tongues in each other's mouths—but I knew I didn't want to do it just because my body was excited. My body gets excited about all sorts of things; deep chocolate ice cream can make me whinny. I wanted to do it with someone who was special. Maybe that's sentimental, maybe in a weird way I'm old-fashioned. So I stopped a couple times right at the verge. I jerked the guy off each time. It seemed the least I could do.

Liam Baker and Elinor Wylie were both occupying my mind, though

I have to say Liam was occupying my body's longings, too. When I woke in the early morning and had some time before I got out of bed, I could feel my private area telling me it could use some attention. I've been massaging my mound for a while and it's okay but it's tacky, too. You feel better some but it's like working out in a solitary sexual gym—me, myself, I. I wanted to grow up and be a woman, not some horny, pathetic teenager. Of course, I would still be a horny teenager but you know what I mean. Getting laid right means you are being loved right.

One problem, as I mentioned, was that half the girls in the school also wanted to get their manicured paws on Liam. I was one of a crowd who made a point of hanging out when he was around and exchanging smiling, lingering glances in the hall and generally flirting. It's not easy in school to be subtle about stuff. School is unsubtle about everything. There are always crowds and you have to be careful about who is around. Girls get jealous fast—like in a second. There's the phone, of course, and e-mail, too, but I have to say I prefer being there in person. Plus guys don't do well on the phone. After a minute or two, you start to sense this dead air on the other side. You can feel they want to start throwing a ball around or do their chemistry homework or get back to *Playboy*. They barely know what gossip is.

At the same time Elinor Wylie was starting to commandeer my soul big time. At first, despite my attraction to how she looked and the mystery of her, I wasn't keen on her poetry. It seemed so stiff, so formal, so decorous. It functioned according to rules that weren't available to me. I knew what rhyme and meter were because school teaches you a few things, but I couldn't get an emotional handle on her at all. I couldn't understand why the rules mattered so much. There seemed to be a sad, large cloud over her yet she never told you why the cloud was there or how it came to be. It was her weather. And it was oblique and always seemed to be looking back at something. Maybe I'm too young to understand regret and maybe regret is the basic stuff of poetry. It felt almost as though she were a figure from a play and that she wanted to be that figure. Each poem was a speech that came from a pose. But I didn't know what the play was about.

There was one poem, however, that grabbed me immediately called "Sea Lullaby":

The old moon is tarnished
With smoke of the flood,
The dead leaves are varnished
With colour like blood,

A treacherous smiler
With teeth white as milk,
A savage beguiler
In sheathings of silk,

The sea creeps to pillage,
She leaps on her prey;
A child of the village
Was murdered today.

She came up to meet him
In a smooth golden cloak,
She choked him and beat him
To death, for a joke.

Her bright locks were tangled,
She shouted for joy,
With one hand she strangled
A strong little boy.

Now in silence she lingers
Beside him all night
To wash her long fingers
In silvery light.

Until I read this poem, it hadn't occurred to me that something could be awful and beautiful at the same time. To use a vocabulary word, it's macabre, which means that it "suggests the horror of death." We tend to try to keep things in black and white: death is bad and life is good; the ocean is beautiful and drowning is terrible. Elinor Wylie, however, mingles her feelings. Part of her exults in the sea's power. Not only that, the sea is a woman. The sea isn't a good girl who is always raising her hand to help out in the classroom and has no dark, moody feelings inside her. The sea is a woman and that's what I want to be. That's what I am.

It's strange stuff, poetry. It can throw a sort of switch inside of you that you didn't know was there. When we do our reports, it's sort of ridiculous because we're supposed to tell what we think the poem means. Mrs. Mansfield is big on meaning. Meaning is like God to her; there's no getting around it. I talked about how Elinor Wylie personified the ocean and how she used vivid language such as strong verbs and how she left you with the final image and how the poem was cruel and lovely at the same time. I talked about the quatrains and how they came from ballads, how tight the rhymes made them. I talked about the tradition of poems about the sea. I could see Mrs. Mansfield beaming with teacher happiness but I wasn't happy. I wanted to talk about how the poem made me feel.

I'm not sure what I would have said, though. And I doubt if anyone would have wanted to hear my feelings in any case. School is like sleepwalking. You don't want someone to be getting too real. No one ever said school is about reality; it's about playing along. You didn't make the whole thing up and you sure aren't going to overturn the whole, habitual cart on your own. So you have to deal. Some days I can feel a vague nausea inside of me. I even think I see it on other kids' faces, even when they're being chirpy and lively and seemingly thoughtless. It's the weariness of having to give answers to worthless questions when you are bursting with questions that aren't getting answered. You're sitting there wondering if some guy like Liam is going to give you the time of day or a lot more than the time of day, and some serious but vaguely pathetic adult is going on about benzene or the Gadsden Purchase or the co-sine of *x* or what Hemingway's fish means. It's dull and ridiculous at the same time.

I think what I might have said about "Sea Lullaby" is that it is soothing to me in the way that a lullaby is soothing. It shows the horror of nature's brute force at work. It shows the indifference we try to cover up. It's very cold but has strong emotion. It's distant but it gets under your skin. The poem is like the sea; it doesn't care what anyone thinks about it. It exists unto itself yet this woman, Elinor Wylie, sat down one day and made it up. On the other end of it there was this human being—the writer. That seems very mysterious to me but again sort of comforting. I'm sure the world was telling Elinor Wylie to be good the way my mom is always telling me to be good. Probably, even though I read two books about her, I don't know the half of it. No book is going to tell you what her mom said when Elinor didn't finish her meal or dropped a water glass or had a bad period. The poem sure doesn't try to be good. "She shouted for joy" is the line that hits me the hardest. That stuns me. It isn't soothing. It's gorgeously violent. Part of me loves it and part of me wants to cry for the little boy who wasn't so much washed away as "murdered...for a joke."

When I was working on the report and reading lots about Elinor Wylie plus reading her poems, my mom told me I was becoming "distant." Somehow my mom wants me to be a faucet she can turn on whenever she wants and out gushes positive feeling. I wish it were that simple. I guess I'm closer to my dad because he doesn't need that. He can let me be. He doesn't need me to show my love as much as my mom does. Elinor was close with her mom throughout her life; they needed one another. I can understand that, though I can't imagine Elinor being demonstrative with her mom. But the old days—I mean the way Elinor looks in her white dress as she stares down—seemed to give people more room. The old days seemed to give people more privacy. Maybe because everyone had so many manners, everyone was careful all the time not to get too close. Or maybe there were walls that were made of feelings between people and you respected those walls. Those walls kept you safe.

I read that Elinor was a debutante, a word that I'd heard but never focused on. It meant that you were introduced to society. "Society" didn't mean the world at large; it meant a select group of people who came from good backgrounds and had plenty of money. I guess as far as the people with good backgrounds were concerned everyone else had bad backgrounds. There were dinners held for young women and teas and dances that were called "cotillions." The dances must have been like proms but nicer. Probably people drank champagne and there was a small orchestra or dance band. There definitely wasn't a disk jockey like at our prom who is some local guy who thinks he is much hipper than he really is. We drink Pepsi and ginger ale because we're underage, though there are always parties around the prom where you can get sloshed.

Trying to imagine what it was like to be a debutante was hard. Why did someone need to be presented? And why did everything about a woman revolve around getting married? You get the feeling with Elinor that she wanted to be left alone. She was sensitive. How could she feel being a piece of good-looking, well-bred meat? I like to dress up and show myself off but I want to do it on my terms. I don't need to be introduced to society; I'm in society already. And it seems so hopelessly stiff with people bowing and making small talk and whispering. You get the feeling that the world would end if someone farted. Of course, Elinor was pretty and everyone was taken with her looks. She was a winner in that way. Yet she knew she had to marry and the guy she wound up choosing was not a good choice. He used to lose it with her, getting mad and frightening her. After she ran off with another man, he killed himself—not a lovely night at the cotillion.

Meanwhile, I was working hard to get on Liam Baker's radar. Maybe I was in no better shape than Elinor was in her debutante phase. I was still a young woman/girl (as in "Girls Room") who was aware that guys called the shots. I got to walk the crowded, ugly halls and listen to that brag talk that guys do to show they are guys, about how this girl goes down and that girl is a scag and similar charming remarks. I never heard that kind of stuff come out of Liam's mouth. He seemed genuinely nice but maybe the guy that Elinor married as a young woman seemed nice to her. You want so much for things to go right with someone that you can blind yourself with your own light. You don't want to be left out. There seems nothing worse than being left out.

I actually asked Liam one day what he thought of poetry. I didn't ask him if he liked it, just what he thought about it. You don't want to make the guy uptight or come on too strong. He said that he hadn't read much of it but what he had read, he liked. He'd read a bunch of sonnets by Shakespeare and thought they were "cool." That's the word we all use endlessly because it helps us over the rough spots where our feelings and lack of vocabulary might drag us down. Even if we have the vocabulary we use it because it's easy and you don't want to show off how articulate you are. We wound up talking about how song lyrics weren't the same thing as poetry. They didn't look so great on the page. They seemed kind of clunky and simple-minded but a poem did look great on the page. Of course, we both knew that Shakespeare was a genius so you couldn't compare him to anything. Liam was going to start telling me about how last year he did his report for Mrs. Mansfield on William Carlos Williams (a poet I hadn't heard of) but Christine Lucas came by and intruded herself into the conversation. She was clearly hot for Liam and had—within the limits of our stupid dress code—some serious cleavage to show him. Somehow William Carlos Williams evaporated.

I must have gone home and read some more Elinor Wylie. I remember that I started to really get her that night. I stayed up late, which is my favorite time because my parents have gone to sleep and the house is quiet since my brother is away at State until he flunks out. I can sit in my room and drink a glass of milk and eat Oreos and swear the next morning to my mom that I didn't make any crumbs that cause ants to appear. I can fantasize about the prom. I can listen to music. After I've done my homework I can read what I want. Elinor had gone beyond the homework category. She wasn't leisure; she was starting to feel like a necessity.

It's hard to say how many times I read this poem over. It's called "Address to My Soul," which is a very Elinor title:

My soul, be not disturbed
By planetary war;
Remain securely orbed
In this contracted star.

Fear not, pathetic flame;
Your sustenance is doubt;
Glassed in translucent dream
They cannot snuff you out.

Wear water, or a mask
Of unapparent cloud;
Be brave and never ask
A more defunctive shroud.

The universal points
Are shrunk into a flower;
Between its delicate joints
Chaos keeps no power.

The pure integral form,
Austere and silver-dark,
Is balanced on the storm
In its predestined arc.

Small as a sphere of rain
It slides along the groove
Whose path is furrowed plain
Among the suns that move.

The shapes of April buds
Outlive the phantom year:

Upon the void at odds
The dewdrop falls severe.

Five-petalled flame, be cold:
Be firm, dissolving star:
Accept the stricter mould
That makes you singular.

Elinor was proud. She was like a princess except that there are no princesses in America. She loved to write about cold and ice and winter. And she never seems really present in her own poems. It's her soul she's addressing but right away you feel the distance. Why would you think of talking to your soul? Isn't your soul right there inside you? What's the need of it?

Yet Elinor clearly had the need to distance herself and distinguish herself. Life hurt her a lot. You can feel that in her pictures. She seems too composed, as though she's wary of taking an extra breath. You can feel it in her words that are engaging but remote, too, that seem to want to keep life away. I had to look up a word like "defunctive," which I learned is obsolete and means "funereal." And there are places I don't really understand, such as what "the universal points" are.

I understand enough, though. She had to steel herself and she was trying to accept that. I think she asked a lot of herself. Each of us creates ourselves and that's one reason why high school is scary because you see that happening in front of you. You see how the kids around you are choosing the roads they are going to go down and how they are ignoring other roads. Elinor created herself through her poems. That seems a little crazy to me but I'm sure I don't understand how much she needed to do that. The poems were more, however, than her need. They were beautiful in their "severe" ways. When I read the lines "Accept the stricter mould / That makes you singular," it thrills me. It's that princess quality. She isn't going to give in to anyone. She's not afraid. Even though she may go to pieces at times, she isn't afraid and she can rally herself, she can bring herself back through poetry.

The poem is full of decorum, which is another word you encounter on a vocabulary test because no one ever uses it. I guess we gave up on decorum. In my school it means that girls can only show so much midriff and chest. And we all complain about it. But for Elinor I have the feeling that decorum was almost life itself. I don't mean the cotillion sort of decorum where you curtsy or whatever stuff they used to do. I mean that she thought life was empty without people being careful and polite with one another. Of course, I know enough by now to understand that people aren't careful and polite with one another most of the time and maybe that's why the poems matter so much. With their neat little stanzas and rhymes and meters, they have a decorum no one can injure. The poem is like a spell or a charm that keeps you safe, like something a princess would pronounce from a room in a tower. Reading the poem aloud in my bedroom over and over, I felt safe.

I wasn't, though. A couple of days later I heard that Liam asked Christine Lucas to the prom. That was that. Christine made a point of being all bubbly and effervescent around me. She had won; I had lost. As for Liam, he was extra nice when he ran into me but we both knew the story. We knew that "nice" isn't going to kiss you hard on the lips. The best "nice" will give you is a peck on the cheek.

It hurt and getting an "A" from Mrs. Mansfield on my report card didn't make it any better. I knew how hard Elinor's life was—with suicides and miscarriages and being made a notorious scandal in the newspapers—and though I couldn't imagine being her, I could imagine that heartbreak could become like waking up in the morning and going to bed at night. It was there and it wasn't going to go away. Even when you were happy and forgetful, when you were swimming or eating Oreos or touching yourself and dreaming about some guy, it didn't go away.

"We're in this for the long haul," my dad says, which is his way of saying that we all die and better face up to it and stick with our responsibilities. Elinor is always writing about death herself. I can't decide if she's inviting death in or keeping death away—or maybe both at the same time. When I sat at the prom with Kenny Peterman who I knew had a crush on me but for whom I cared zilch, I had a sense of what a long haul life could be. I let him get to first base because I didn't want to emasculate him totally but that was it. I walked up the stairs to my bedroom a very intact virgin. I saw the pile of Elinor books on my desk and I thought of her. I wish I could have talked to her.

John Berryman, b.1914

Probably you're thinking that I learned about John Berryman in college because where else would you learn about a guy like John Berryman? You're not going to see his poems on billboards or in local newspapers next to ads for septic tanks and snow tires. No one is interrupting a TV show to do a John Berryman commercial. Et cetera. The fact is I did go to college for two years before I quit and I took a course that had some poetry in it. Our professor was a woman who told us we only were going to read women writers because the guys had gotten too much of a say already. It was ladies' night, so to speak. I didn't go to the class much. To tell you the truth, I didn't go to many classes at all. When I was there I listened to her talk about the male hegemony. You can see that I'm educated because I used that word, "hegemony." I can't say I use it with the people I work with in the carnival because no one would know what the fuck-all I was talking about. Still, that's what professors are paid for—to know words like that. I could dig it. Even if I was a guy, I didn't begrudge her. I didn't turn in any work and I didn't pass either. And I didn't read anything by John Berryman.

By that time I was thoroughly anti-social, to use a phrase my Aunt Marie, who liked to label people because it made her feel superior, was fond of. Not criminal, mind you. I'm not a violent man. I would go along, however, with her description of me as contrary. I'm sure you could get psychological and consider my "pathology" (a word that excited Aunt Marie). Everyone is always explaining everything but it doesn't change anything. I mean people go out and do what they do. Have you ever heard someone say, "Hey, I'm not going to do this because I know what's causing me to behave this way?" That's not any human being I ever knew. It sure as hell isn't anyone who works with me running the Ferris wheel or selling cotton candy. They'd fall over laughing if someone said something like that. No one is going to, so they're safe.

My old man was a drill sergeant in the army so we moved around a lot. I guess you could have said that he was contrary if you think that a son of a bitch is contrary. I never looked at it at that way. He was being what Uncle Sam wanted him to be. You've got a bunch of chowderheads and you've only got so much time to turn them into working, military units. The problem was he didn't leave his job at the office. When he barked at me about picking up my stuff or not saying, "Yes sir," to him or putting my feet up on the couch or a hundred other dumbass things, I barked right back at him. I wasn't much for sucking up. Those vanilla kinds of words never felt good in my mouth. If you aren't going to speak your mind, I don't see the point of being here.

We disagreed about everything you could disagree about. It drove my mom nuts. She would start screaming about why she ever had kids. She really meant why she ever had me because my kid sister was Goody Two Shoes. She seemed to come out of the womb that way. That's what I mean about looking for explanations: nature has some cards in her deck that nurture doesn't understand. My sister was always on her best behavior; everyone cooed over her as if she were some kind of little minister. Life being life, she was a hypocrite who made fun of our parents behind their backs. Such are the ways of good people. They'll praise God but hate their neighbors, give to some charity but sneer as they walk by a homeless woman on the sidewalk. I send a postcard to my mom every now and then but I'd never send my sister one. You can grow up in the same house as someone but you sure don't have to like the person. Proximity can make the heart throw up.

The sugar got my old man, plus he had wicked high blood pressure from yelling at people all the time. He even barked in his sleep, telling those sheep to jump in double-time over those fences. The sugar runs in my family; it'll probably get me, too. That's why I might as well do what I want while I can. When he passed, my mom said, "Well, I guess you won." What a shitty thing to say. It was a game between my dad and me. We took it seriously and we didn't much care for one another but we agreed to keep on playing. Even when I ran away (which I did a couple of times), I was playing a game with him. We were professional spoilers, he and I. We knew that about each other. Mom was an amateur. She was forever harping about peace begins at home. How someone who wanted peace could live with someone who trained men to kill is beyond me, but most things between men and women who stay with each other for any period of time are beyond me. We assume that fornication is communication but it's not true.

I never got around to registering for the draft because my old man was gone by then and I didn't want to get my ass shot off in some place I couldn't so much as pronounce. Whenever I asked my old man about something political, he would say that was how it had to be and I'd better learn to live with it. He was big on that way of thinking if you want to call it thinking. It seemed to me that if you were choking, you might want to spit the wad out but not to my father. He believed in swallowing it, whatever it was. He didn't know squat anyway because the only things he read were the sports pages and the funnies. His favorite topic was how Negroes were getting paid too much. "Here I am busting my ass every day to keep this country from becoming a communist trough and these niggers are getting paid the big money to stand there and hit a ball." He was a racist scum so I naturally became a liberal. I didn't have any colored friends because just when I was starting to get comfortable in whatever school I was in we got our asses hauled to another base—military gypsies. I used to shoot baskets with a couple of colored guys in Washington State and they seemed like human beings. I'd figured that one out already. There wasn't much that my father wasn't wrongheaded about.

It's hairy sometimes with me being a liberal because we travel in the carnival through the South and the South is one crazy place. I'm talking about the sixties when things started to change and the white people didn't want those things to change. All these sorry-ass characters you would have at the county fair who didn't look like they had anything in the world beside some beat-up car and their prejudice. You could hear them babbling while they were waiting in line for ride tickets or hot dogs about four on the floor and fuel injection. You'd think there were cosmic differences among the pieces of metal that got turned out on some freaking assembly line. Their poetical tee shirts spoke for them—"Heavy Chevy" or "Damn Dodge." Talk about pathetic. Since I was a Bozo, one of those clowns who taunts people, I had a field day. "You don't look like you have the money to buy a tricycle, buddy." "You don't look smart enough to put the key in the ignition." I could go on for days. I did.

The racial stuff, though, was truly crazy. I thought plenty of times I was going to incite a riot. There's a fence between me and the person throwing the ball to hit the target (which is out in the open) that drops me into the water—Drown the Clown. There were times when guys started to climb that fence. Sometimes their friends pulled them down but sometimes their friends started climbing, too. I knew the cops weren't crazy about what I was saying but we had our own people around and they weren't particular about how they treated someone who was trespassing on our property. You could always pay the police off if one of our guys got a little rugged. They were paid off already—it was part of doing business—but they acted as though their racial prejudice was a matter of conscience, that they couldn't allow someone—"a nigger-loving Yankee"—to say such things in their county. What frauds they were.

The cool thing about the carnival is that as long as people are spending, I am free to shoot my mouth off. No swearing, of course, due to the youngsters and Methodists strolling around but I didn't need to swear. I had more than enough words without swearing. "Hey, Darktown, what was your momma up to?" It was a rare sucker who didn't bite for that one. At first, the guy that I had singled out would look around to see if I was talking about someone else. I'd nail him again: "You, buddy, the one who's looking around like you don't know who I'm talking about. Don't be ashamed. There are some great colored people in this world. Look at Martin Luther King. He's an inspiration." Needless to say it was a segregated fair. God forbid that Negroes should be around eating the same cotton candy and squealing on the same rides. The world might have ended if that had happened. I noticed that when that world did end, the planet kept spinning.

"What the hell did you say, clown?" Not many people are good at thinking on their feet; a question gives them some time to compose themselves. If a girlfriend were there, the stakes were higher. She'd be hanging on the guy's arm; you could see she wanted to see what sort of man he was. I figured she was probably a spiteful, racist bitch so sometimes I went after her, too. When the guy asked me a stalling question, I would come right back at him. "People don't speak English down here but you understood me. You got those dark Negro eyes." It freaked them right out because I could pick the whitest of white guys and start in on his eyes. They never thought about their eyes. Why would they? I knew it was ridiculous but I knew their fear and prejudice were ridiculous, too. The worst thing about it for them was that I wasn't all worked up or anything. I was doing my job; I was stating the facts. It was personal what I was saying but it sounded impersonal. Didn't they hate that?

The sucker would be sputtering, calling me names, fishing for money to put down to pay for balls to throw and drop me in the water. I kept it up: "You probably don't have two nickels to your worthless name. Borrow some money from your girlfriend." Usually they threw wildly. I had a half-million phrases to describe what a dignified old carnie I knew called "errant tosses." That wasn't a phrase I used. It was more like "You couldn't hit the fat lady's behind." Not the most creative stuff but it worked.

Being a Bozo you learn that once you get under someone's skin, you can set up shop there. As a drill sergeant, my dad must have known that. I'm not giving orders but what I'm doing isn't that different from what he did, not that he would be proud of someone who dodged the draft and taunts good old boys for their hateful ways. For all his bile, though, my old man kept his eye on the prize. He knew how far to push the needle. You get a feeling for how much a person can take and when the person starts to lose interest. With the suckers on the midway you can tell pretty fast how many dollars they are willing to plunk down. You're looking for a sign that they've reached their limit. Sometimes it couldn't be more obvious. They hit the target, I fall into the water; they dismiss me with a taunt and split.

Sometimes it's money that stops them. Money runs deep and someone has to be real upset to forget about money. I pride myself on making that happen. Sometimes it's the person (usually a woman) who's there with the sucker who is embarrassed or pissed off about what a spectacle the guy is making of himself and wants him to get the hell away. You can see her tugging on the guy's sleeve, trying to get his attention and get him out of there. I go after that, too: "Don't listen to her, Mister. You probably don't anyway, right?" "She's only taking pity on you, Mister. Don't pay her any mind." Sometimes I get a couple of extra bucks this way because any guy who listens to a woman telling him what to do in public is no guy. That's one of the Ten Commandments of being a guy. When the guy starts scowling at his girlfriend as if she were his mother, I've made a sale.

Most guys don't hit the target and leave with a muttered complaint or a dumb threat about what's going to happen later in the parking lot. If not much is going on, I give them a parting shot but usually I'm on to the next mark. You have to keep searching the crowd, which is more work than the banter, which becomes second nature. I like that part of the job, though, because it keeps me lively. I already have the big picture about people, which is that they tend to be jerks (and I don't exclude my Bozo self) but then you have to do the choosing. You can see a true loser five miles away, though sometimes they are so lost they don't even respond. That's embarrassing, sort of like kicking a crippled dog. They stare at me with empty eyes. It's pitiful.

What I like are the more confident guys who take it as a challenge, the guys with a few shreds of sanity and self-respect. If I can get them mumbling, it makes my day. At first, these guys will smile a little smile at me, like "Well, this guy is a doofus so I might as well prove it to him. This is what the carnival is all about." He's right. The carnival is about separating people from their money and making them feel more or less okay about it—though if you ask me the whole society is about that. So one of these guys gets the baseball and I start in on him about how he looks like he's Mister Cool but really he's a wimp who can't throw any better than his retarded sister. You have to understand that my line of work is not about human kindness. Once in a real long while, the guy turns out to have a retarded sister or something close to it and starts to foam. Whether he does or doesn't, I keep pimping him on and that's what intrigues me, whether the guy who keeps missing can put the balls down and walk away or whether the guy gets mad. You'd be surprised at how many guys who look pretty together lose it.

This all has to do with John Berryman, though being a famous poet he probably never worked in a carnival. You never know. Carnival people don't fit the stereotype of the boozer who's on the lam from the law. I've met one or two of those but I've met more reformed boozers who like what newspapers call the "lifestyle" of it, the freedom that goes with not being tied down. Roots are overrated. There's a lot to be said for not waking up some morning and wondering what you ever saw in the town you've spent your life in and the person snoring next to you.

I'm not a travel agent, though. What you see traveling around America in terms of scenery is okay but not that fascinating. Probably there aren't many people who make a point of visiting every county in South Carolina. As one of my mentors, Tex Thomas, told me, "The carnival is about geography, boy. You better start to learn it." Tex was a lifer from New Hampshire who ran a food concession with his wife Doris and thought he was a sage. I've learned that you often have to indulge people to live with people.

I encountered the poetry of John Berryman when I encountered Ruthie Mae Rogers. She was one of those Southern, two-first-name girls. I have to say I liked that right off. It makes me feel I'm getting more woman than I bargained for which is how I like women. They come with two breasts so they might as well come with two first names. The carnival had a day when we had pulled down but didn't have to take right off. Someone had screwed up something about the next fair. Or maybe some sheriff was unhappy about the Bozo he had heard about and wanted more money to keep law and order. It turned out that Doris had an aunt in the town we were in (it was in South Carolina) and that this woman wanted to meet some of the "carnival folk." She promised some home cooking and that always sounds good. The carnival has its own cook but even a peasant like me gets tired of hamburgers.

Ruthie Mae had blue eyes with a lot of glittering green rays in them. You don't see that color much. When you see eyes like that it's not uncommonly a woman who has all the flames on the stove turned up full blast. That would have been Ruthie Mae. She came up to me and said that I didn't look like a carnie. What was I doing traveling with the carnival if I didn't look like a carnie? She said I looked like a hippie store clerk.

It wasn't a great way to meet somebody but it got better. Actually I didn't have to say much because Ruthie Mae liked to talk and seemed to have had no one who was semi-intelligent (which is how I would categorize myself) to talk to for months. She told me she had been to school for a while up north and that she was going to go there again and that she was just about dying with "boredom and frustration" (her words exactly) from staying with her aunt who was a decent woman but too much of a decent woman. "She's always prayin'," Ruthie Mae said as though she were talking about someone who went around shooting guns off or knocking doors down. It wasn't a good thing all that praying, which, of course, I agreed with when she paused for breath.

After I made sure I had enough of some real tasty fried chicken, I was invited up to her bedroom but it wasn't for the purposes of sex. She was explicit about that. "Don't think you are going to start ballin' me here and now just because I am lonely." She wanted to read me a poem by a "crazy, Yankee, lecher poet." I was all ears. That very day an irate sucker had called me—and I'm as blond as it gets—"a rotten little Dago." Kind of sad when people can't even get their slurs straight. So I could stand this, too. I sat on the edge of Ruthie Mae's bed, a dented metal thing that looked as though it had been thrown out of a third-story, college dormitory window, and she read to me in a tight, high voice, as if she were sort of happily drowning, one of the *Dream Songs* by John Berryman:

> The high ones die, die. They die. You look up and who's there?
> –Easy, easy, Mr Bones. I is on your side.
> I smell your grief.
> –I sent my grief away. I cannot care
> forever. With them all again & again I died
> and cried, and I have to live.
>
> –Now there *you* exaggerate, Sah. We hafta *die*.
> That is our 'pointed task. Love & die.

—Yes, that makes sense.
But what makes sense between, then? What if I
roiling & babbling & braining, brood on why and
just sat on the fence?

—I doubts you did or do. De choice is lost.
—It's fool's gold. But I go in for that.
The boy & the bear
looked at each other. Man all is tossed
& lost with groin-wounds by the grand bulls, cat.
William Faulkner's where?

(Frost being still around.)

Ruthie Mae looked at me fiercely after finishing the poem. "Do you know who William Faulkner and Robert Frost are, carnival boy?" She tossed her head like a filly. She had a good head of curly, brunette hair.

I told her who those two writers were and she asked me how come I wasn't "a dumb asshole." I didn't answer that question and after a short silence she started lecturing about the poem. Since my life in the carnival revolves around speaking, I'm fairly good at remembering what people say. In this case, Ruthie Mae told me that what she had read me was a real poem. A real poem didn't have to be beautiful. That was foolishness and for high school girls. A real poem came from the soul. "Course," she said, "it comes from a man's sex and a lady's sex, too." She smiled sweetly for the first time since we had met. "But it's not just that. It's the words. You don't have to worry about what the words mean exactly. It's not like that. What you have to do is let the words carry you so you can feel their current. It's like an electric current but it's like an ocean current." She paused as if pondering what she just had said.

"What are you doing here in your aunt's house in South Carolina?" I asked her.

"What are you doing in the carnival?" she asked back.

"Groin wounds," I said matter-of-factly.

She looked at me in an interested way. "All men have groin wounds from what I can tell."

"You ever meet this poet?"

"I heard him read his poetry last year. He's got a sort of gruff voice and a beard. You can tell he drinks too much. He's got way more feelings in him than he knows what to do with. Even with writing poems he's got way more feelings." She was keeping her eyes on me. "Probably, you've never been to something like a poetry reading."

She had me there. "When you're with the carnival, you do what the carnival does."

She came over from the chair she was sitting on and sat beside me. "I don't know if I want to go to bed with you but you are right nice looking. I like that long blond hair. I was just kiddin' when I told you that you looked like a hippie store clerk. You don't mind if I touch that hair, do you?"

Ruthie Mae traveled with me for a few weeks. That's the longest I had ever been with one woman. I wouldn't say we got along especially well but she read me poems by John Berryman and I have to say I liked that. For Ruthie Mae, reading the poems seemed to be something powerful yet calming as if she were tapping into some signal that came from the center of the universe. I say that because a fair amount of the time she was like storm clouds gathering in the west. You could see it coming and it was going to rain down on you. Buying her an ice cream cone or telling her how beautiful her hair was didn't make any difference. I was all right with that because I didn't have any great expectations about us living together happily ever after. Our bodies liked each other; I was pleased enough with that. I got plenty of winks and smiles and slaps on the back from some of the older guys. I didn't tell them she was reading poems to me. There are some places it's best not to go with people. Poetry seemed one of those places.

I came back one day to the cubicle in the trailer where we were living and saw that she had cleared out. It made me sad, I had to admit. I liked being with a woman every day and smelling her womanly smells, the perfume and lotions and the fishy smells, too. I liked reaching over in bed and feeling a woman's body there. I even liked her mess—bras and underwear and tee shirts wherever she dropped them. My dad and mom were neatness freaks so I've always been partial to people who are slobs. Ruthie Mae didn't give two shits about being orderly. She wiped her lips with the back of her hand. When she burped, she seemed downright glad.

On the unmade bed was her copy of John Berryman's book, *77 Dream Songs*. I stared at it for a while. I wasn't going to cry or anything but I wasn't unmoved either. Just because you're a guy who spends his days taunting other guys about their manhood doesn't mean you're a stone. I knew she treasured that book and she left it to me because she thought I deserved the book. It was something to remember her by but it was something that mattered in its own right. I read pretty much whatever came my way because a number of people in the carnival were big readers. A lot of what they passed on to me was crap—you wouldn't believe how many different kinds of written crap there are—but some of it wasn't. Needless to say, no one had ever passed on a book of poetry to me. There are limits to everything but Ruthie Mae had little use for limits. I admired her spirit and hoped it wouldn't incinerate her.

I remember holding the book and feeling that it might start jumping up and down right in my hands. That's not so foolish as it sounds because I already had gotten to feel that poetry wasn't anything to treat lightly. Whatever you thought about this John Berryman—and a number of poems that Ruthie Mae read were Greek to me—he wasn't fooling around. Even when he was fooling around in his clever, full-of-words way, you knew he wasn't fooling around. He didn't sit and write poems because some boss was telling him to turn out more poems for the poem production department. He was writing them because he had to write them. I liked that. Most people seem to me like they are just here for a vacation on earth. They're looking around and making their remarks but they don't really seem to be here. They're just out on the midway gawking. They don't seem to get that it's a one-way ticket. It was real clear that John Berryman wasn't here on vacation. Plus he was horny all the time and made no apologies about it.

What really got to me when I started reading the poems was that Berryman had these characters in the poems. One is a guy named Henry and then there is this other guy who is never named who refers to Henry as "Bones." What's going on between Henry and the straight man who calls him "Bones" is quite a bit of weird, Negro-and-white-man stuff, that back and forth kind of patter that minstrel shows used to do—except they are talking about what we are doing with our lives on earth, more or less, or more specifically how fucked up the Henry guy is. Some of the old timers in the carnival remember minstrel shows real well. One guy told me he really misses it, how funny the whole thing was, these white guys putting on blackface and talking like Negroes. To me it seems like more crazy, American, racist shit. It kind of makes my skin crawl to think about it. It really makes my skin crawl to think about an audience of thoughtless white people sitting there and laughing at it. I see those people every day and I know who they are. I know how easy-going evil can be.

What impressed me a bunch was how Berryman was willing to step into the sea of hurt that divides white people and colored people. He went right after that weird, deranged jive-talk and made it his own. You knew he was saying that this is crazy but it's a kick in its way and I'm going to play both sides of the street. It's a real uncomfortable feeling but then you wonder about how people used to listen to stuff like that and think nothing of it. That kind of took my breath away because I knew that while I could have my fun on the midway making money for the carnival, I'd otherwise better keep my opinions about race to myself. Some of the carnies made no bones about how they would never work with Negroes. Even the thought of it seemed to agitate them. One guy named Ripple Red who could have picked me up and broken me in half used to go off about how Negroes weren't fit to shine his shoes. That was funny because I never saw Ripple Red in anything but these beat up clodhoppers no self-respecting shoeshine would get near but that's how it goes. People pump themselves up with bad wind.

I liked the language that Berryman sort of invented for what went down with Henry and Bones. It wasn't like a language anyone really spoke but it still sounded like a language someone could speak, someone real smart, real wired, and real unhappy. I thought about it because I was out there every day spieling to people. He was spieling, too. There's one poem in the book where Berryman is talking about how not much has happened in the South since things supposedly got integrated. He writes the poem in Negro dialect but he's not writing in that dialect to show you how stupid Negroes are. He's writing in that dialect to show you how full of shit white people are that they want to hold on to their racist grief. The last three lines of the poem are the real deal:

> But I do guess mos peoples gonna *lose*.
> I never saw no pinkie wifout no hand.
> O my, without no hand.

When you hang around poems for a while you start to see that every little thing matters. You see that he uses the dialect in the next to the last line—"wifout"—but then in the last line he uses the regular word because he's going to a different place in that line. He's thinking that there's more hell to pay and that it's no joke. It makes you think about a phrase like "long hand of the law," for instance. Poetry shakes your head up about words. I liked that.

Though the carnie people would never give Berryman the time of day, they would probably get along with him, at least the old-timers who weren't stewed in racism. That's because Berryman writes the way these guys talk, kind of staccato-like but also old-fashioned. When I first got taken into the carnival, I didn't know half of what the older guys were saying. What was a "clem" or the "tip" and how come they didn't say "barker" but "spieler" or "talker"? As a spieler myself, I caught on fast; I could see that the carnie language protected us from the straight world, the clover kickers and the hoosiers. I think that was some of what Berryman was looking for. He wanted words to protect him from people in the straight world so they couldn't boil him down the way my Aunt Marie boiled everyone down. "Oh, John Berryman, he's one of those poet types," she'd say in her fruity, nasty voice as if he were some phony who wore a trench coat to bed. At the same time—and being a Bozo I could get with it—he was telling people to bring it on. As the old-timers liked to say, he was "screwed, blewed and tattooed." It was what my poetry professor would have called a "paradox."

It's not like I lack for courage; every day I heckle guys who are a whole lot bigger than I am, to say nothing of being angry and bitter. What the poems have done is amp me up. I don't want to get bored out there and some days it feels like that because when you get down to it people are pretty predictable. What I've started doing is some of the patter that Berryman does, some of that blackface shit. The craziness of America is much bigger than I am. I might as well start swimming.

It upsets the men folk of whatever-the-hell-county pretty strenuously. Last week I was out there on my perch above the tank and I saw this tall, swaggering guy with one of those cut-off tee shirts so he can show off his muscles and I knew he was my man. On his arm was this little honey blonde who looked as though she'd stepped out of a sorority house. Sometimes I can just feel my anti-social juices flowing. Sometimes I almost get excited when I see such a good, miserable thing coming my way.

"Mistuh Clown, you see dat big, red-faced man ova dere?"

"How could you miss somefin dat ugly, Mr. Bones?"

"Well, dat fella thinks he's smarter dan everyone else."

"Dat right? Dat hunk o' blubber?"

"He thinks he can hit dis target in one pitch and drop me in de drink."

"He couldn't hit his nose wid his right hand."

The guy sidled over and gave me a look that was supposed to wither me like defoliant. "Clown," he said in a voice that was meant to show who the boss was, "you are going to die." I like that when they escalate the whole thing. Falling into some water when you have a wet suit on underneath isn't exactly death but you let them say what they want to say. It's their language, too.

"Mistuh Clown, you ready to die?"

"Bones, if it takes me outta dis town I am. I heard all de Negroes moved away because dis town was so low-down."

I could hear a murmur in the tip. One second I was just going after Mr. Fraternity, but the next second I was going after all of them. They started sparking on the guy and telling him to make sure that he hit that Yankee clown. Who the hell did that clown think he was?

The guy wasn't a bad pitcher but he kept missing about three inches to the left. I could have pointed this out to him and counseled him to change his stance and point of delivery but people were pressing dollar bills on him like they were going out of style. No use ruining a good thing.

"Dis white boy just won't give up will he, Bones?"

"De Souf is gonna rise again, Mistuh Clown, and when it does dis man gonna still be throwin' baseballs."

He never hit me and walked away frowning a big-time frown. The sorority sister was frowning, too. I had the feeling she might be rethinking her choice of boyfriends. White Hunk wasn't all he was cracked up to be. Everyone was pretty sullen which gave me a boost but I was busy lining up the next clem. You never want a lull. I picked a little guy in a natty sport coat. He looked as though he couldn't throw a baseball five feet.

"See dat genleman ova dere in de lovely coat, Bones."

"Dat lil genleman? De one who looks like if he drank too much water he might disappear?"

"One and de same. Well, he can hit dat target, can't you, suh?"

The carnival teaches you a lot of things, one of which is to take life as it comes. Some days it's going to rain and no one is going to show up. Some days the sun is going to shine but the tip is full of Baptists who wouldn't dream of paying their God-blessed American money to drop a clown into a tank of water. And some days are golden—one clem after another steps up to the counter. I don't think John Berryman was very good at taking life as it comes. If the poems I've read are any indication, he was pretty bad at it. I think he and Ruthie Mae shared some of the same stormy weather. He made something of it, though, and you have to respect that. It wasn't one-way. He made his own lightning.

I've met other Bozos from other carnivals and they are some real bent characters. If you tell it like it is, you probably are bent. If you do it in public, there's no question about it. If you go after the worst darkness in people like their twisted, vicious hatred, you are signing on for trouble. I imagine I shouldn't extrapolate—to use another college word—from John Berryman to talk about all poets past and present. Still, if you asked me what a poet is I'd say it's someone who believes words can draw blood. Any Sunday idiot can make nice. Somewhere in the warm Carolina night the spirit of Mr. Bones is alive and well—"roiling & babbling & braining"—and pissing off the hegemony.

Weldon Kees, b.1914

When I was growing up in Nebraska in the years after World War I, my mother often admonished my wishes or desires with the tart words "make do, Alice." If I lingered before a store window display, she would hiss, "New isn't better." We weren't poor; my father was a lawyer who dickered in business propositions throughout the state and sat on the boards of three banks. My mother, however, came from stark Scandinavian poverty; what she knew best was scrimping. Restriction was a vestment she wore gladly; it went with that immigrant desolation in her that always was wary, always expecting misfortune around the sunny American corner. When the Depression came she shook her head wisely, confirmed in the sagacity of her distrust. I scolded my improvident dolls when they clamored for new dresses. Then to my mother I voiced some modest yet impossible longing. Back and forth I went—pulling strictures out of me and then putting them back in.

I'm old now, seventy-eight; I feel like a cottonwood branch that has fallen to earth and dried and bleached in the summer sun till the sap is clean gone. I am sere. When I think back to my high school days with the poet Weldon Kees, it doesn't seem possible that this slow-moving assemblage of bones is part of the same lifetime as that bounding, giggling girl-becoming-a-woman—but such are the wonders of oblivion. I'm tempted to launch into highfalutin language when I start thinking about Weldon, because poetry is nothing to sniff at. Like our heart, it's built into us. Poetry makes you feel how your moments are a kind of music, how something as dull-witted as time can be articulate. There's no age when a body doesn't need that.

It's true that not many poets hail from Nebraska's small towns. I speak as someone who is writing on a typewriter at the kitchen table in an ancestral house (as much as anything is ancestral in Nebraska). Though its middling destiny is bred in my brittle bones, I have no interest in mocking my home state: these bones are going to rest in its black soil. That's why biography is tricky. You never know. You wouldn't bet on someone as cosmopolitan and passionate about poetry as Weldon coming from these silent plains. You might not bet on my ancient typewriter and my arthritic fingers caring to write this, but verisimilitude is obtuse and genius like Weldon's is wayward. It's as if someone had to take that vast, dark, cyclone sky and put it inside of him. Someone had to see beyond and through the dwarfed, hopeful streets that designated civilization. Someone had to believe in the big cities and then give up on them. That was Weldon Kees, who was—to quote his words—"notched in darkness."

Though he wrote humor pieces and stories and sketches that were printed in the school newspaper, I thought of him even then as a poet. It wasn't the satirical couplets he wrote that are the stock in trade of any clever boy or girl who can make words jump through hoops; it was his instinct for poems. When he read a favorite aloud, you felt that in speaking those words he was touching a place inside himself that was electric. When we dismiss adolescence as the yeast that settles into the dough of adulthood, we condescend. We slot and bracket those rich, demonstrative feelings when sirens call from rocky yet sublime heavens and each day is a year. The quicksilver passion of poetry forms a natural mirror. What the young person feels in the rhythms is the burgeoning pulse of his or her life.

It went without saying that our town was unremarkable, though Weldon would have been inclined to add "lethal." Much like the weather that contained ungodly extremities—tornadoes, blizzards, thunderstorms—there were imbalances (culture or its lack of being a large one) yet life, like the sky, added up to a benign torpor. We sat in the center of the nation. Everyone worked hard and believed in work, yet life was unhurried. Weldon would have written "dull." Especially those of us who grew up within the town proper accepted the porches, ice cream socials, gliders, picnics, and choir practices as part of the landscape. We had, my Norwegian grandfather used to say, "become civilized fast." Though our manners weren't quite Victorian—we knew what jazz was and followed the movies avidly—they might as well have been.

We were living in a bubble of sorts, a long, sweet, sheltered moment. Perhaps, these decades later, an earnest young man is reading "The Lady of Shalott" by Alfred Lord Tennyson to an earnest young woman, but I doubt it. Too much has happened. I know because of what happened to

Weldon. I know because of what a strain it has been to pretend that nothing happened, that all is forever well and safe in the fabled heartland. Look at the tablet for the war dead, most of whom died on the other side of the world. Perhaps in their last moments they glimpsed the orderly streets and modest buildings and the endless sky above them. I like to think such a vision might have comforted them. I suspect that Weldon would have laughed ruefully, that laugh of compassion that wants to deny compassion.

I still can recite the whole of "The Lady of Shalott." I can't vouch that such a skill has held me in good stead. I don't recall anyone ever asking me out of the blue if I cared for poetry. Even if someone had and I told him or her the truth, it probably would have merited a polite shake of the head and a mild, indulgent smile. As a woman I could claim the famous feminine weakness for feeling. With its intensities and lucid mysteries real poetry—not the Joyce Kilmer stuff—leads a secret life. I could accept that because not long after my days with Weldon I realized that I was a woman who loved women. Nowadays that's nothing to shake your head about, although I wouldn't walk into the local Methodist church and start lecturing on the topic. Back then it was scandalous. My mother raised me to not call attention to myself; it was part of making do and perhaps that was just as well. Though it's been tenuous at times, I've made it through life without having my spirit shattered to irreconcilable pieces. I couldn't say that about Weldon. The current gospel is to be open with everyone, as if frankness were an automatic good, but honesty isn't that simple. Mysteries, heartbreaks, and depths—the fabric of poetry—remain.

Probably you know Tennyson's poem's opening stanza:

> On either side the river lie
> Long fields of barley and of rye,
> That clothe the wold and meet the sky;
> And thro' the field the road runs by
>   To many-tower'd Camelot;
> And up and down the people go,

Gazing where the lilies blow
Round an island there below,
The island of Shalott.

Those lines are beautiful the way I thought Weldon was beautiful, though I never told him that. "Handsome" is the word and Weldon was that, but he was beautiful, also. His eyes were dark, fiery pools of feeling. They drew you in but you had no idea as to what you were falling into—not that I, as a young woman, cared. He had fine black hair, pale skin, and he dressed very neatly. That was the era when young men were still expected to dress like gentlemen, when not everyone had decided to become "natural" or "casual." Even in high school he had the air of being composed and purposeful. He was proud.

Weldon possessed a good, sturdy, masculine voice. We'd sit on a creaky porch swing or on parlor chairs whose massive oak arms smelt of furniture polish and recite poems to one another. Tennyson was our favorite. We wished to be enchanted; the great poet accommodated us. He couched his fine words in a measured cadence; that grave lilt that for me is a hallmark of verse. Weldon came to write a lot of what is called free verse—the United States being a higgledy-piggledy place—but he never lost his feeling for the lilt. The cadence; "on either side the river lie"—was an emotion that possessed you like a spell. I felt when I listened to Weldon that the steady sway of the words could go on forever. I felt a quiet power that left me elated and weak.

Tennyson's words spoke for a wraith-like world yet were precise and solid—"the red cloaks of the market girls." Some were consciously old and consciously poetic. They weren't daily, spoken words. The world they evoked never was and never would be. Young people take to such a world because their own is so confused yet full of possibility. Soon enough the castle gate will come down but while it stays up the vision of other worlds where ladies are fair and knights are brave seems just and kind. Such a vision had nothing to do with our Nebraska, and that was the point. The Lady about whom we were reading was "robed in snowy white / That loosely flew to left and right." No store held that robe; no money could purchase it. The newspapers trumpet the discoveries of modern science but there are other kinds that are as important. To experience a legend that speaks to the heart is a very big discovery.

Though the poem would qualify as airy, it was about men and women and the power that the attraction between them holds. The stanza when Lancelot appears is unforgettable:

> His broad clear brow in sunlight glow'd;
> On burnish'd hooves, his war-horse trode;
> From underneath his helmet flow'd
> His coal-black curls as on he rode,
>   As he rode down to Camelot.
> From the bank and from the river
> He flash'd into the crystal mirror,
> 'Tirra lirra' by the river
>   Sang Sir Lancelot.

Lancelot is a man with a capital "M." Though I've loved women best it never canceled my feeling for the male presence. I think the world works best when the masculine and the feminine are both allowed to have their ways—that means men to women, women to men, men to men, and women to women. I'd hate to live in a world where only one direction worked. I'd hate to live in a neutered world. The words Tennyson chooses to render Lancelot aren't special ones, but they are deft. The notion of Lancelot's forehead glowing or the sight of his hair makes you feel that this is a man in his unreduced form. This is a man who is proud of his body and the love and power that his body holds.

When Weldon declaimed this stanza, I felt that Lancelot was there before me. How could I not? There is something wonderfully artful in Tennyson's beginning the second part of the stanza with a prepositional phrase. Perhaps I sound like a school teacher but it's true, isn't it, how you are focused on Lancelot and then the poet takes you away from the image of Lancelot and makes you feel the place where Lancelot is and how Lancelot's song makes that place come alive? For the space of one line—"from the bank and from the river"—you lose sight of Lancelot but he returns. Lancelot himself is the river. How can the fated Lady not look? The little syllables of his song feel like the oldest of sounds, gentle nonsense that makes deep sense, the passion of beauty, that pure exultation of being alive.

For those minutes that were the speaking of the poem aloud, we were in that world. Rhyme is a childish toy but it pleases in the quick way that rattles and jacks please. To rhyme the likes of "day," "gay," "say" and "stay" isn't a great leap. Still, the charm holds:

There she weaves by night and day
A magic web with colours gay,
She has heard a whisper say,
A curse is on her if she stay
    To look down to Camelot.

The awkwardness of rhyming, as in putting the adjective after the noun as if English were French, makes for an odd grace as things get said in ways they normally would not. To make a whisper say something is eerie. The word "say" isn't necessary. That's the point, though. The whisper is alive and that's what poems do—they make everything come alive. Yet within that vitality, there is death. "Singing in her song she died."

People who kill themselves (or who are presumed to have killed themselves, as was the case with Weldon's leaving his car by the Golden Gate Bridge one July day in 1955) are judged according to that one act. Their lives fall into a single-file line that leads only to death. Those left behind ponder the void and search for premonitions. I can't say that I have succeeded, for though I was half in love with Weldon and took in his every motion, I never felt that he was morbid, that he dwelt on death to the exclusion of enjoying life. He knew it existed and that may have made him unusual for his age. My mother's mother died when I was little but my memories were scant. Death was a distant story. Weldon, however, showed an uncanny glint when he came to the poem's end, where the knights who have gathered around the boat "cross'd themselves for fear." You could feel pity in his voice and an edge that felt like contempt. Death was terrible and real. I remember looking away from him; he frightened me.

Since it is something made by a set of perishable hands, the poem seeks to overcome death. Each stanza's refrains offer a certainty that never recedes. There is Camelot and there is the Lady of Shalott. They go on and on as Tennyson keeps weaving the refrains through the "magic web" of each stanza. They insist; they insinuate. If I didn't know what happened in the poem, I might feel that mere words could ward off harm. Perhaps, though, it's more that they cause harm—"Who is this? and what is here?" Weldon once said to me that you could feel how confident Tennyson was of God's existence. It didn't surprise Weldon that at the end of the poem God was called upon. I remember telling him that it surprised me, that these knights and ladies didn't feel at all like the Christians I knew. He laughed and said that no poet wanted to be a Christian but had to make the best of it. As a virtuous maiden, I told him I wouldn't tell a soul what he had said.

You might be wondering where our bodies were amid these lulling and tumultuous words intoned by our softly throbbing voices. Sometimes we were a chair apart and sometimes we were right beside one another. There were moments when I was tingling with something for which ecstasy seems as good a word as any. I wrote that I was half in love with Weldon and I wasn't being coy. The other half of me was in love with poetry. We were acolytes receiving great, avid glimpses. Without the poems we were who we were—I a shy, gawky girl with an insistent yet muffled intuition about my sexuality (not a word in my vocabulary then) and Weldon a wit waiting for a subject. The poems made credible the funny couple that we were. In modern times, people prefer to look down, but poetry is aspiration. It gives you wings.

Our ardor wasn't sexual. Ardor is feeling for feeling. Ardor is delight.

We felt the hovering presence of sex—how could we not?—but grabbing hold of that presence was tricky. You have to understand what life was like back then. Sex wasn't slathered all over everything the way it is now. Sex wasn't being advertised and discussed publicly and filmed in every nuance. The times that Weldon kissed me (and he did) were moments when a bridge appeared into the land of passion. Yet quickly, we both withdrew.

I've thought about it forever, our hanging back. As upright young people we were raised to hang back and we took that upbringing seriously. We were moral about measuring a teaspoon of sugar or cleaning a dish; every action was judged. We knew our bodies were unruly. We knew to beware. Plus, I knew however obscurely I had fantasies and feelings that went beyond the acceptable. Those statements are accurate and daunting but some part of me has never been convinced. I think that while poetry brought us to a certain place it kept us from moving on. There is a famous passage in Dante where two lovers share a book and then forget their book as they give themselves up to their love. We never forgot the book between us. We only knew one another through what we shared—the impossible ground of poetry.

Unlike the prairie around us, that ground wasn't limitless. I have the feeling I am talking about no more than a half year. I knew even then, even in that straitlaced town, other couples who were in the coarsely scintillating phrase, "doing it." Yet I would no more have had sex at that point in my cloistered life than I would have hopped a freight train to Colorado. We had Lancelot and the Lady and the fineness of their mysterious feelings. Tennyson thinned out some very thick emotions. Although it would be easy to make fun of us as idealistic, it would not be fair. It would be fairer to say that we wanted to be somehow larger than the young man and woman we were but weren't very sure who that was in the first place. Weldon's lips were beautiful to me but more beautiful were the ones I imagined the Lady had.

Every enchantment posits disenchantment. The great, bearded, Victorian poet whom I still read understood that well. Beauty exists in relation to the cankers of woe and mortality. We come to know that it can't be otherwise, but Weldon knew that because he wanted to know that. Whether it was a politician or a movie star or, closer to hand, a teacher or shopkeeper, he had a nose for the gracelessness of ineffectuality and pretension. The adults Weldon mocked and mimicked were more or less amiable Americans and harmless if not downright pathetic. Yet there was something hard in Weldon, something that insisted on being restless, something that refused to accept our Midwestern good nature.

You expect a bright boy such as he was to leave a small town. It has no prospects for a shrewd tongue. To stay would have been to turn against his own self. Weldon's leaving, though, went deeper than that. What I watched from afar in his adult life was said well in one of his poems—"Cold, cold, a great gray winter entering." Weldon wanted to understand that winter. He hungered for the harm of it. A genius of negatives, he had to know the worst the world could tell him: "I watch the snow, feel for the heartbeat that is not there." Or "No one, she says, and rocks, and coughs...." As much as he couldn't abide credulity, he adored absence, perhaps because even the high school boy I knew was an unhappy person who sensed that disenchantment would offer him a crooked, counterfeit happiness. He would be the one who was not deceived. I like to think that he didn't resent the enchantment—he remained a poet—but he titled one of his books *The Fall of the Magicians*. Weldon was all about that fall.

The irony was that I was the one to go, at first, far away. Wendell went off to a small college in Nebraska not far from home. I went to Massachusetts. If I could have convinced my parents to send me to Europe, I would have. That was impossible; to a young woman from Nebraska the Pilgrim state of Massachusetts was the next best thing. As if it were a sweet or a scent, I craved history. I needed to feel that my life was part of the long flow of time. I needed to feel that generations had gone into the making of a college. My mother told me that I was a snob but that wasn't true. I felt bereft. Relatively settled though it had become, the bareness of the landscape in which I grew up alarmed me. What were people and their little buildings to this vast, silent prairie whose grasses grew and died, grew and died? When I went for walks on my grandfather's farm, I could feel the emptiness, how it cared not a jot for the staunchest human efforts. I could feel that the people, for all their hammering and sweeping and planting and tending, were doomed to paltriness. I was Weldon's confederate, I suppose.

He congratulated me in his stylish, snappy way, praising my choice to go east as a sign of intelligence. He smiled his brilliant smile and told me he was glad I was getting out. We both knew what that meant. His words weren't hollow, but I heard in them a glimmer of mockery. I had made a simple decision; I had chosen a definite identity off the shelf of identities—Seven Sisters College Woman. Weldon would not make such a decision. The Tennyson who purveyed idylls and legends and ballads seemed a very equable man but Weldon, though he groused about it, loved the hurly-burly, modern world where a poet was not likely to be equable. Though I was standing with him in the main hallway of the high school, I sensed that already Weldon was far beyond me. He would refuse the easy consolations. I walked the few blocks home in a daze and lay on my bed. My heart ached.

As a connoisseur of misdirection, Weldon would have enjoyed that my going east was the cause of my returning west. "Why had I bothered to go in the first place?" I can hear him asking. To return after having tasted the fruits of a larger civilization would have seemed criminal to him. And how could I have explained it? It wasn't that I didn't like the east for I liked it very much. Every day that I walked through the campus of Smith College, I felt that I was among the voices of the past and the medley that constituted the great, present moment. Generations of women had preceded me. I felt a solidity that was reassuring: there are such places and I am living in one. Sometimes I stopped and simply stared at a building or gate or walkway and exhaled. There were students who liked poetry as much as I did—a few even more. I was part of something that wasn't precariously perched on the vast edge of nowhere. And I found I could love a woman and it was beautiful.

Yet I returned promptly, not because a job waited for me or because my parents importuned. I returned because I wanted to live where I came from. Many of my classmates headed to New York City or Boston to begin their first jobs or attend to their new husbands. They were as excited as fledglings about to leave an uncomfortable, confining nest. I, who carried the majestic, plains sky inside me, couldn't see myself living in something even as modestly urban as an apartment building. I couldn't see myself looking down at cars and pedestrians or taking an elevator or going into a subway or walking down a long hall and putting a key into a lock. I wasn't afraid of those cities. It was more that they felt awkward to me, like wearing an extra layer of clothes on a hot day. They seemed too close for comfort.

I had no plans to take over my grandfather's farm or raise horses or even assist a local vet (all of which I wound up doing). I was a little embarrassed and more than a little forlorn when I showed up with my diploma and suitcases and surveyed the lack of prospects. Was I merely timid? How could I conceal my love for other women? Had I swallowed so much history back east that I had lost my geographical senses? Did I see myself as a prophet of sorts, a bearer of a superior education, a missionary? During the first weeks home, I wrote a letter to Weldon trying to explain myself but never mailed it. He had his own problems.

Though I wasn't sure as to what I was going to do back in Nebraska, I was aware that the march of history—Crash, Depression, Hitlerism, Bolshevism—echoed everywhere, that there was no sanctuary. Perhaps because he was so sensitive, Weldon didn't want there to be history; it got in his way. He wanted the twenties when we were growing up to go on forever. He wanted to live in an era when artists were free to be artists without history in the form of dictators or haywire economic systems or ideologies soaked in blood making a mess of everything. He was happy to rail at history, but he didn't want history to rail back at him. Making art was a right that history shouldn't impinge on. Now, as an old woman who has seen too many headlines, I wonder if there is any greater idealism.

That cocoon in which we grew up was a bittersweet remembrance. When I came upon Weldon's poem "1926," I memorized it immediately. I needed to have it inside me. To say that it compelled me would have been an understatement. If it wasn't exactly my life, it was close enough to make me shiver. As poems go, it's as good as anyone's:

The porchlight coming on again,
Early November, the dead leaves
Raked in piles, the wicker swing
Creaking. Across the lots
A phonograph is playing *Ja-Da.*

An orange moon. I see the lives
Of neighbors, mapped and marred
Like all the wars ahead, and R.
Insane, B. with his throat cut
Fifteen years from now, in Omaha.

I did not know them then.
My airedale scratches at the door.
And I am back from seeing Milton Sills
And Doris Kenyon. Twelve years old.
The porchlight coming on again.

The poem is a long, almost infinite way from Tennyson. Yet perhaps Weldon would have felt, as I feel, that it isn't so long. What is timeless enthralls. The moments we perceive in childhood have that quality because we have yet to construct a chronology of our selves. For a while, "my life" is a relatively short tale. Opposing the ego is the timeless nature of unencumbered being—a porch light coming on, an orange moon, a dog scratching at a door, what occurs once and again and again. The child has no control and must accept that. Even a small-town neighborhood is vast.

"Then" and "now" make for the saddest of songs and the one Weldon loved best. We know there are miseries in store for us. Tennyson etched a beautiful one when he described the Lady in the boat—"A gleaming shape, she floated by / Dead-pale between the houses high." Such romantic visions weren't permitted to Weldon; he was of our bright, lost world. Yet he knew what enchantment was. It was, among other things, the world of the movies, two of whose stars he named in his poem. It was the world as it existed in its own right. It was the precision of anything and everything, how the instinctive architecture of being rejects formlessness. Adults must forgive the wide-eyed child. It would be an even sadder world if they didn't. The softly grave "I did not know them then" says that.

As in Tennyson there is a refrain. What Weldon's poem begins with, it ends with. There is deep comfort there. It is false, of course, but, nonetheless, it is deep. Poetry can have it both ways; that is why it is poetry. It enchants and disenchants at the same time. In the common word "again" there is an entire world. The child is taken care of; things are as they should be. Recognition and habit and custom make life sweetly precise: early November is the time for raking leaves. That the poem is titled with an actual year is more than the custom of autobiography. Weldon pins time down in order to grant its ever-moving due. The stillness is magical. This world cannot be, yet it is. It can't stop haunting those who are willing to feel it.

"Twelve years old," wrote the poet and the inference is that a small town is best perceived through the eyes of a narrator who is that age. Unless they want to be grotesques, it is no place for adults to live out their lives. The actuality of the small town at the moment Weldon perceives it isn't oppressive. It's almost beautiful in its ordinariness. What happens to the two people whom Wendell chooses to put into the poem's central stanza is horrendous. There were other neighbors, it goes without saying, to whom ghastly things did not happen, but it would not have been in Weldon's interest to represent their humdrum pleasures. He wanted the stern contrast and there it was. Nostalgia was a lie that memory told to reality; Weldon would have none of it.

The poet came back to Beatrice to visit his parents, John and Sarah. I glimpsed him a few times, going into a store for cigarettes or a newspaper. I could have gone up to him and seen that lovely smile once again, for I am sure he would have smiled as he whistled my name in mock incredulity. I ran into his parents now and then and could have gotten an address or a phone number or told them to make sure Weldon gave me a call the next time he was in town. I didn't want to, though. He had left; I had stayed. The equation could not have been starker yet the life I staked out for myself was as odd as his was. I became the horsewoman who never married and was treated by the men as almost a man. The married women were warier; they suspected I did not want to be one of them. They suspected there was more to me than my talk of saddles and foals and they were right. I knew what a secret life was and I knew the pleasure of its secrecy. According to the unofficial laws, a person such as myself shouldn't exist, yet there I was.

I followed Weldon's progress through the literary thickets. After a time his name appeared in publications that if not well known in Beatrice could be had through the mails. *Time* magazine was more than well known; it was famous and Weldon worked there for a time, though "toiled" might have been his word. He was not a respecter of grand enterprises. They were bound to compromise too many people in too many ways. He understood the modern succubus that as it excites people grinds them to dust. I read stories and reviews and poems; I bought copies of his books when they came out. No one in Beatrice knew what to make of Weldon but that went without saying. Here was an ironist who had grown up in a place that prided itself on its plainness and friendly manners. Anything oblique was a threat to our way of life. Even a woman like myself who disappeared occasionally to another life was part of that "our."

Though it was unfair, I came to feel sorry for Weldon. Not for his difficulties as a writer—I respected him for persevering and succeeding in the many ways he succeeded. What I felt sorry about was Weldon's hunger. He wanted stimulants and if it has not been good at anything else the century has been good at creating stimulants. Weldon couldn't stand the lackluster manners of small ponds. He needed to feel he was an important, creative person among other important, creative people. I didn't begrudge him that. What saddened me was how Weldon seemed trapped in a play of his own devising. He always wanted to be moving on but there seemed nowhere to go. Small-town America already had failed him. Its big cities were amusing and exciting but what was there beyond amusement and excitement? Weldon certainly didn't want what most people in those cities wanted. He wasn't interested in getting ahead in any conventional sense; he was not going to head a business corporation. He wanted cities in which a poet could live as a poet—not as a professor or a writer of ad copy or newsreel scripts. I don't think those cities existed.

To me it seems that poets' lives are chosen for them, that they are legends of a sort. Each genuine poet is a page that comes to life from the book of possible legends. Weldon's is the Man Who Was Not There. The character Weldon created, "Robinson," is that man:

> The dog stops barking after Robinson has gone.
> His act is over. The world is a gray world.
> Not without violence, and he kicks under the grand piano,
> The nightmare chase well under way.
>
> The mirror from Mexico, stuck to the wall,
> Reflects nothing at all. The glass is black.
> Robinson alone provides the image Robinsonian.
>
> Which is all of the room—walls, curtains,
> Shelves, bed, the tinted photograph of Robinson's first wife,
> Rugs, vases, panatellas in a humidor.
> They would fill the room if Robinson came in.
>
> The pages in the books are blank,
> The books that Robinson has read. That is his favorite chair,
> Or where the chair would be if Robinson were here.
>
> All day the phone rings. It could be Robinson
> Calling. It never rings when he is here.
>
> Outside, white buildings yellow in the sun.
> Outside, the birds circle continuously

Where trees are actual and take no holiday.

To be remorseless and bemused is an exacting fate. I can hear the world saying, "Well, what's his problem?" His problem is that he exists but isn't convinced of it, doesn't care to be convinced of it, is indifferent intentionally to the signs that are provided. Our Tennyson was a good, responsible, English songbird of a poet. Weldon's song was more like an ache. Perhaps for a time the words made the ache go away. People who say that words are good for nothing are fools. Words are blunt tools and sometimes fine ones. They can't heal, however, what doesn't want to be healed. They can't cut through habitual disappointment.

If I sound censorious, I apologize. Weldon was a star I guided my own life by. He became distant, a rumor of sorts, but I knew that the joking, Tennyson-spouting boy was the genuine article. I knew him in a way New York or San Francisco could never know him. I could imagine the great, nagging question: how do you make a place for what is precious, particularly when it doesn't want to announce itself, particularly when it is at pains to signify it is not a hoax or entertainment or charade but the real, gripping thing? Weldon's love of understatement was Midwestern as was his grit. He wasn't going to get tossed off the horse of life. He would throw himself off but he wasn't going to get tossed off.

Though I promised myself I wouldn't do it, I'm talking about what I assume to be his death. I'd guess that anyone who knows someone who has taken his or her life is bound to wonder whether something could have been done. Maybe a letter from me saluting my high school poetry mate would have cheered Weldon up. There was someone in Beatrice beside his parents who kept a scrapbook of clippings about him. There was someone who didn't look puzzled when the words "modern poetry" came up. There was someone who spoke proudly of our native son without adding any raised eyebrow qualifiers. But I am just sticking pins in myself. None of that would have mattered.

If I had a wish, it wouldn't be for a happy ending for Weldon because there could not have been a happy ending. What I would wish is that I knew Ann, Weldon's wife. To have been married to Weldon seems extraordinary. I don't mean that Weldon was strange or a freak. I mean that he had to have been demanding and difficult but gentle and funny, too. What a wife would know would fill a book, but it would not have been so much what she could have told me about Weldon as what she could have told me about herself. I chose to live an unorthodox life in an unremarkable place. I chose to keep my heart close to my chest. Ann chose to live with a man who was dangerous, who was driven by an unhappy vision, who was selfish. She had to have had her own female courage to bear up under his withering whimsy. Despite their drollery those poems weren't games. And in the end it didn't work out between her and Weldon. It must have been too hard. She loved what was impossible.

Weldon created a spell but it was a harrowing one. It had the authenticity of someone who loved poetry but realized it must measure up to the frightening times in which poetry existed. You can say that Weldon wasn't the man for that task. You can say that the task is irrelevant, that poetry is bound to sing its personal songs regardless of what the world does. I know when I looked at pictures of the atomic bomb, I thought immediately of Weldon. He knew what was in people—"Darkness, blue veins, and broken leases." That was a heavy load to carry through life. Particularly when he knew he was no exception, that what was in everyone else was also in him. I lie in my bed and repeat lines of poetry to myself. It is 1926 and we are both children growing up in Beatrice, Nebraska. The porch light is coming on again.

Anne Sexton, b.1928

I missed the Age of Dylan Thomas and I regret it. I would have loved to have had that fleshy, cherubic, schoolboy body roister in my bed. I would have loved to have had those fat, frank, pendulous lips kiss me anywhere they wanted to kiss me. I would have loved to have felt his whiskey, cigarette mouth on my own mouth. And I would have loved to have touched that thick, sweetly demonic, magnificent tongue—the very tongue of poetry—with my own tongue. I could put exclamation marks after each of those sentences, but a series of exclamation marks is like a line of tired cheerleaders. To feel the weight of that disheveled, word-struck flesh upon me would have been bliss. And to feel his cock throb, heave, and spend itself inside me would have silenced words.

"But, but, but..." the qualifying voice of reason (which primarily would be my mother's) hastens to add. The admonishing finger that points to the sad ending of the bloated, roaring, alcoholic poet is smugger than it is wise. Being ever right about human debility is self-defeating: we all know that the flesh is weak and one, beautiful, earthly day we go under the hill. As Dylan testified, the joys of poetry are joys of the flesh. For me, pining in my carpeted, cutely wallpapered, Jewish-suburban-girl bedroom, Dylan Thomas was the first of the joy-scouts, a precursor of the delirious, angry, sensual sixties. A great formalist, who knew that in art form is everything, he derived from the ancient, chthonic sources of poetry. He pushed the words further than they ever had been pushed before—not in some painfully modish way—but as the life force expressing its stricken, passionate, confused, importunate self in words. He was splendid in the root sense of that word (poets are addicted, rightfully so, to etymology)—that which shines. He took on the splendor, the carmine luminescence that is at the core of language. His rhythms mimed the great leap that is made by each word as a sound tries to conjure a thing—or less than a thing, a notion or dream. He was the heat at the root of language. Nothing grows without that fine heat. This planet would be lifeless without it.

I missed Dylan, but I didn't miss the one-night stand with a poet of my choice. I believe in moments of truth—that's why I teach and write poetry. I believe in the power of sex, too. However fleeting, a sexual encounter, particularly one between two more or less strangers, is a moment of truth or a failure of truth. Even when their bodies are joined as one, people may avoid each other. It's rare sex that isn't mixed with some importunate dose of fantasy. However much you want to feel the other person's body and however much you do feel that body, you still are in your own. Mind mingles with flesh until a compound is at work. When someone cries out, I trust the body's knowledge.

A poem, as it reveals a sensibility colliding with the mortal facts, is also a moment of truth. Although the moments must pass, the black and white of the poems remain. Shakespeare wrote more than one immortal sonnet about it. A poem is a frail eternity and must consider itself in that unforgiving light. Poets know how thin the paper is. It must not deter them, however, for poetry is an embodied mystery. It is the dark woods and the dark night and whatever light—splendor—is able to illuminate those shadows. It goes further than that, though, because, as some very serious poets have noted, poetry is playful. It exults in the mouthy hullabaloo of language and in its own long-standing vitality. Dylan Thomas knew that sweet clamor as well as he knew the sea outside his window or the winding streets through which he ambled.

My capacity for jumping into bed had its limits, but I wasn't about to miss out on a good thing. If you don't enjoy your body when you're young, that's sad. I was young in the 1960s as they turned into the 70s and I was glad and proud to be a woman. That's why I'm writing this about Anne Sexton. Though I never met her, she meant everything to me, even more than Dylan because Anne was a woman who met womanhood straight on. For that I could never thank her enough. I believe that poets are shamans who do the work that must be done for other people to live in the world. The United States of America wouldn't know much about shamans, but then the USA doesn't know much about a lot of things, one of them being poetry. Anne, who on her good days was a very canny woman, understood that but plowed ahead. You can call it obsession or bravery or self-delusion or sheer craziness—boiling down a person to a motive or a trait depresses me. What matters is that she did the work; she wrote the poems.

Whatever jerks they may be—and plenty of them have been—the poets I have entertained have, at least, done the work. I respect them for that. Creating a poem has been compared to numerous processes but in all metaphorical cases it's about making and what making entails. That means it's about the first jet of inspiration that could be tiny or large but comes from nowhere and takes hold of you. Then you have to know what to do with it. Of course, you don't know, how could you know—but you have to try. To me, a Jewish woman who is dangerously close to being an atheist, to disregard the calls of imagination is sinful. Though I shouldn't be using the word, the imagining feels holy. Feeling your way into the poem is like opening the door of a shadowy room and groping. You're not even sure about the floor underneath you—it's likely not to be level—nor are you sure when you start to touch some objects—which represent feelings because every image is expressive—what they are. But it's your room, that's the main thing, and you come to learn your way around it even though it always remains dark except for that splendor that lives in laying out the words. Though a poem often is a little thing, twenty lines or even less, a good one is sturdy and knit together like bone, ligament, and muscle. The poets themselves are often not so sturdy.

I teach at a liberal arts college in the Midwest and for many years have been in charge of inviting poets to come to our college and read and talk to a class or two. I am the college's token poet and accordingly we put on some token readings. Despite their infrequency, there is each year much grumbling from the faculty about our spending money on people of whom no one beside me has ever heard. That they have not heard of any poets is my fault—not theirs. To a person, they have better things to do than follow the travails of poetry in latter-day America. Once I would have written "even the English department feels that way" but somewhere along the hermeneutic highway the English department turned into anthropologists of culturally determined texts who argue among themselves about how those texts are to be interpreted or not interpreted. They have X-ray eyes and see through everything except jargon. Poetry is eschewed as another once-privileged remnant of the Age of Backward Thinking. To my impulsive mind, they are dreary people who lack the sense to know they are dreary—the worst kind of Puritans. That, of course, is the last thing they think they are.

Fortunately, the school's higher ups think poetry readings are part of the cultural atmosphere a college should maintain along with a glee club and an occasional forum on a recent international horror: poetry, madrigals, and genocide. Though she never makes it to a poetry reading or a talk on Rwanda, I have seen the college president at the glee club concerts. Being Jewish, I am there, too. I get a thrill out of attending a Christmas concert and humming along. Some illicit pleasures never wane.

I was brought up to be a Good Jewish Girl who would no more hum "The Little Drummer Boy" than she would hang a St. Christopher medal on her automobile's rear view mirror. Being a Good Girl is a category that transcends religion and even race, but the Jewish spin is daunting. To me it's pure hypocrisy. Jews are like most religions: sons are better than daughters, though there is a lot of hooey about what a blessing a daughter is, how being second-rate is okay. Still, it's hooey. Patriarchs outrank matriarchs any day of the biblical week. We all know sex-wise who God is. Women are breeders and a necessary evil. Why, I wondered, as I was growing up, all the anguish about what is inferior? If daughters were to be suffered as creatures who could go wrong in more ways than could be counted, why not bear it with something like grace? When I was younger, I caterwauled but received no answers. From my mother I received shrugs; from my father I received loving, dismissive nods.

The troubling message I got was that I was either on the way to nowhere—unmarried and childless—or to disaster—seduced by a Gentile. One way or another, marriage was the linchpin, but I couldn't grasp what it was the linchpin of. My parents' marriage must have been happy at some point. There was a wedding picture of them displayed on the coffee table in the living room beside the glass dish filled with Hershey Kisses that no one ever touched. They were smiling and looking properly resplendent in their 1930's garb. The picture said, "Look, we are doing the Right Thing. We are getting married." Decades later their marriage seemed to me not so much bad as indifferent, not so much requiring radical surgery as subsisting on the antacids of resignation. That's a lot of bad meals and I think both my parents would have wearily agreed. Time had done something quietly awful to them. Was this what I should welcome?

And why in any case were the dangers so luridly presented to my younger sister and me over and over? I realize that Jewish Anxiety is the eighth wonder of the world and has kept three generations of American comics gainfully employed, but we started out as good girls and despite occasional lapses we didn't, as children, stray far. I had the feeling that however good a girl I was, it wasn't good enough. I had the feeling that if my mother could have turned my sister and me into nuns she would have. Maybe that was the problem: Jewish girls couldn't become nuns. For the simple fact of being female was a problem in itself and there was no way out of that one (sex changes hadn't been envisioned and would not have been considered Kosher in any case). We bled, we cried, we pouted, we were fools for love. We weren't just the weaker sex or the other sex; we were the impossible sex.

When my sister and I would get into a spat, my father would call my mother to referee. "You know what they are like. You're a woman." With his face about to dissolve into an ugly shriek of exasperation, you would have thought the combined forces of Jezebel, Ishtar, Delilah, and the temple prostitutes were confronting him. My mother groaned and started wheedling us: "Don't you girls know what happens to bad girls? Do you want to be bad girls who wind up on the Bowery with nowhere to go and no one to love?" We stared at her with saucer eyes. Where did she get such stuff? From trashy novels that good girls weren't supposed to read in the first place? From her mother who had worried about her turning out to be a bad girl? We lived on Long Island and barely knew where the Bowery was. Rather than face any more conjectures about what might happen to us, we stopped arguing. Gratified, my mother beamed at my father.

When I discovered the poetry of Anne Sexton something very deep inside of me went "Hallelujah!" It wasn't that Anne was showing me the way out of being a woman. It was that Anne was showing me the way into being a woman. It wasn't by giving up on men or becoming aggrieved or self-righteous or making excuses or hopeless accusations. It was that Anne marched through the supposed swamp of womanhood and didn't miss a step. She didn't stop to make discriminations about what she should be feeling. She kept moving and in her metaphors that were like fireworks of the heart she kept describing what she was feeling. Whatever the feelings were, she made them part of her poems—shame, pride, fear, exuberance, lust, regret and on and on. I liked that "on and on." Having feelings was not a rolling-of-the-eyes curse; it was a gift. The emotional errands on which she sent poems were genuine ones. I would never minimize how much shaky darkness was in Anne, but I was okay with that. At least it was real and not some fabrication meant to frighten girls into being automatons. Bad Jewish girls could learn from Gentile girls. As far as I was concerned that was a biblical illumination.

I knew there had been women poets before Anne. As one species of Jewish Bad Girl—the un-maternal—I didn't plan on having children, but if I did and had a girl she would have been called "Emily." The original Emily, though, had to stay in her room to write what she wrote. It was clear that men—no doubt like my father in their suspicion of women—were not going to take her seriously. They looked down on her from their assured peaks of male self-importance. Emily kept on writing. She didn't burn her poems or stuff dolls with them. She kept them because she knew she was doing important work. It was work she must have enjoyed, but it was work. She was clearing a place where women could be women and be recognized for the kinds of insight women could have. She wrote some genius poems; in their jumpy blend of the domestic and the cosmic they were poems that a man never could have written.

I respected other women poets, but it was as though I was waiting for Anne to show up. The very accomplished likes of Marianne Moore or Elizabeth Bishop seemed finical when compared to Anne's generosity and temerity. They were acute, but they hovered at a certain distance. To me there remained about them something that seemed ladylike. The irony was that Anne in being a woman was unladylike. Or it might be said that women before Anne were stretching the permissible elastic. Anne snapped it. Anne did the unthinkable. She accepted and rejoiced in the female body.

When in 1969 I read Anne's poem entitled "In Celebration of My Uterus" I started to hyperventilate. People talk about how a poem can physically affect you and they aren't kidding. I remember feeling that hunger I felt when I had a new book of Anne's in my hands. I remember very specifically buying my copy of *Love Poems* and starting to read at random and finding that poem:

> Everyone in me is a bird.
> I am beating all my wings.
> They wanted to cut you out
> but they will not.
> They said you were immeasurably empty
> but you are not.
> They said you were sick unto dying
> but they were wrong.
> You are singing like a school girl.
> You are not torn.
>
> Sweet weight,
> in celebration of the woman I am
> and of the soul of the woman I am
> and of the central creature and its delight
> I sing for you. I dare to live.
> Hello, spirit. Hello, cup.
> Fasten, cover. Cover that does contain.
> Hello to the soil of the fields.
> Welcome, roots.
>
> Each cell has a life.
> There is enough here to please a nation.

It is enough that the populace own these goods.
Any person, any commonwealth would say of it,
"It is good this year that we may plant again
and think forward to a harvest.
A blight had been forecast and has been cast out."
Many women are singing together of this:
one is in a shoe factory cursing the machine,
one is at the aquarium tending a seal,
one is dull at the wheel of her Ford,
one is at the toll gate collecting,
one is tying the cord of a calf in Arizona,
one is straddling a cello in Russia,
one is shifting pots on the stove in Egypt,
one is painting her bedroom walls moon color,
one is dying but remembering a breakfast,
one is stretching on her mat in Thailand,
one is wiping the ass of her child,
one is staring out the window of a train
in the middle of Wyoming and one is
anywhere and some are everywhere and all
seem to be singing, although some can not
sing a note.

Sweet weight,
in celebration of the woman I am
let me carry a ten-foot scarf,
let me drum for the nineteen-year-olds,
let me carry bowls for the offering
(if that is my part).
Let me study the cardiovascular tissue,
let me examine the angular distance of meteors,
let me suck on the stems of flowers

(if that is my part).
Let me make certain tribal figures
(if that is my part).
For this thing the body needs
let me sing
for the supper,
for the kissing,
for the correct
yes.

I felt so exhilarated that I was faint. I was in my student apartment with its posters of Janis Joplin and Bessie Smith that looked out onto a frowsy, winter backyard of dead grass, but I was first of all in my body. My body had been a matter of grave concern to my parents, a sad weight, particularly what in high school my girlfriends and I called the "delta" in our little homage to Anais Nin. "How's the delta doing today?" we'd ask in the way guys would ask other guys how it was hanging. Why not, I kept thinking, exult in my body? What was wrong with being in a body? Were we Gnostics, people who despised the flesh? I knew from more than one Jewish wedding that my parents could whoop it up with the schnapps-drinking best of them. But there was a cloud hanging over us girls, the cloud of the delta.

Anne didn't free me from guilt about my having a woman's body. I did that on my own and I had men to thank for it. They wanted to use what I had and I wanted to use what they had. It was a utilitarian bargain, but it was ever much more than that. It was about appreciation. I liked being appreciated. I liked being Woman with that capital letter. We came in all sizes and shapes, but we all were Woman and Anne got that so right. That long passage of anaphora—to use a word I teach in the college—where she describes various women is, for me, one of the most beautiful affirmations of being a woman. It's so like Anne to note that they "all / seem to be singing, although some can not / sing a note." Anne didn't make things out to be better than they were. She didn't have to because she was so physically in touch with what actually was. She reveled in it and the metaphors she conceived (for that is the word) were endless ways of praising what is. Maybe since she experienced so much anguish she could praise the body without reservation. She wasn't about to take it for granted. Everything was a gift that could be taken away. Or that she could take away in her grief.

Part of me wished that I could share Anne with my mother; I tried haltingly a few times, as in "Listen to this poem, Mom." My mother would be polite; after all I was her daughter who was going to become a professor and then who became a professor. Education excused many shortcomings. But for my mother the poems might as well have come from Mars. "She's not very polite," my mother would say. "Does her mother know she talks like that?" "She may be a famous poet, but I wouldn't want you to become famous doing that." For every poem my mother had a sensibly prim comment. To her Anne seemed one more example of how hopelessly confused America was, how it insisted on making the private into the public. I would sit in her kitchen that was so much her domain tapping my fingers on the side of the glass of cranberry juice she had given me ("I read it's especially good for women"). "Thanks for listening, Ma," I would say. More than once I wanted to cry. I loved her and knew she loved me. What we could share, however, seemed so paltry, so hedged in by a thousand unnecessary cares and worries, so joyless.

Anne's poem was a "celebration" and that was part of what took my breath away. What others ignored or tried to forget, Anne shoved to the head of the line. It's been said that poets have a portion of the child in them and Anne certainly did. Although she was a grown-up who was assailed by grown-up woes, there was something in her that insisted on pointing a wondering finger and exclaiming. There was something in her that held onto the talk that little girls make with their dolls, that cunning yet soothing commentary about life that as girls turn into women almost inevitably gets lost. Anne wasn't fey, the way for me e. e. cummings was fey with his balloon man and spring. I could feel the self-consciousness of his delight and didn't much care for it. Anne was simply and startlingly direct: "Hello, spirit. Hello, cup." I could have kissed her many times over for her lovely courage.

As a woman I didn't want to walk away from my female courage nor did I want to walk away from tenderness. It was easy for me to advocate for my body's pleasures. Most men (the ones who weren't in a hurry, at least) were keen on performing and if getting me off was part of the performance that embellished their manhood, they were ready to try. If both people can acknowledge how sex is reciprocal selfishness, then each can acknowledge the other—my pleasure is your pleasure. I could say the word "orgasm" without compunction. I had my mother's fearfulness to thank for moving me in that explicit direction.

Tenderness, however, was more equivocal. It took some trust, some openness, and some unfeigned sensitivity. Poetry appealed to me as a place where the intimate dearness of life could thrive. It seemed like an embrace where you could feel someone's heart beating on your heart. Yet even when it was direct, as Anne could be so dazzlingly direct, it acknowledged how oblique its sayings were, how it existed as a series of gestures that never could be totaled up to make a balanced, workaday sum. Every assertion a poem makes—"The sky today is a lackluster blue"—is tentative because it exists in relation to the other assertions that the poem makes. How things hang together in a poem is a matter of great delicacy. The world at large tends, in this regard, to content itself with greeting- card sentimentality, but the hand that writes a poem has to have tenderness in its nerve endings. That hand must feel the fragility and strength of the human pulse. That hand is a great deal more than being a functionary of the head.

I've been looking for a man—he could even be Jewish—who has that tenderness. Everyone knows about guys writing poetry to get girls to think they are sensitive so they can lay them. I met a few of those guys during my undergraduate days and like an idiot fell for them. With time I could see through them: considering that their brains were in their cocks, it wasn't difficult. In the long meanwhile, I've taken what comes my way. I've still got a pair of nice- looking legs but in my prime I drove to the airport to pick up the visiting male poet in a mini-skirt (visiting women poets got a much longer skirt from me) that rode up less-than-demurely when I sat. Since I knew what the poet looked like, I'd be there to greet him at the gate. After small talk about the trip and luggage and the Midwest, we'd be driving down the road in my red Mustang (not a Good Jewish Girl's car) and he would be aware of my legs and thighs. How much he registered that awareness was an arresting situation.

When it comes to sex, guys aren't the most complicated creatures. My heterosexual poet passengers tended to fall into one of three categories: the No-I-Don't-See-Those-Legs, the I-Sort-of-See-Those-Legs-What-Does-It-Mean, and the Bring-It-On. Each group had its own psychic terrain. What the unseeing often meant was that the guy was nervous. Here he is meeting a stranger in the middle of what to East and West Coast types is Fly Over Land and there are these legs to look at and the professor seems okay with him looking at them. A lot of these poets are academics; they know that it is strictly look but don't touch unless you want some ugly, you-don't-respect-the-principles-of-feminism suit on you. But those legs look very touchable. So the simplest thing is to act as though you don't see. Or with some guys they aren't so much nervous as unbelieving. These are guys who have been hard at it in some relationship that gave up the sexual ghost years ago. They are out of practice. Their homing devices are rusty, although I often could feel that their gears were starting to crank. There was promise there, as opposed to the guys who simply are out of it. Asexual poets are pretty rare creatures, but a few fell into that category. Self-love cancelled the need for another body.

The middle category tended to be the biggest talkers. Poets tend to be oral and some are real mile-a-minute men. So they're talking around and through and over and under the legs. They're throwing out hints about whether I like this poet or that poet to get a feeling for, so to speak, the lay of the land. They don't want to offend me at this point, that's for sure. They haven't been on the ground for long, but something important already seems at stake. This is where I ask them the question that I pose to every visiting poet, male or female: "And what do you think of Anne Sexton?" If they don't like Anne—and a few prissy types have grimaced before answering tepidly—I don't leave them by the side of the road, but I know I'm in for a short night. Their poetry reading better be good. Most do like Anne, however, but that's only the beginning. I want to know why they like Anne, what is it about her. The guy's trying not to look too hard at my legs and he's trying to think. He doesn't want to think too hard, though. It might spoil whatever seems to be happening.

What I find with a lot of guys is that talking about Anne lets them put down their male loads (at least figuratively) for a few minutes. They don't get misty—there's nothing misty about Anne—but they do get real. They like her almost gallows humor; they like her sexiness; they like her honesty but the deeper ones, the ones who have been fishing in the lake for a while, will talk about how Anne went somewhere that they as guys know they are never going to go and that they understand that. Put at its simplest level—women are not men. They start talking about how they adore the female body (the legs, the legs) but they don't know what it's like to be in one and how the feelings that come out of that body can be, to them, both incredible and moving and how Anne was both of those things—incredible and moving. I'm aware that they are to some degree playing up to me, but I am also aware that they aren't. For some seconds the legs are almost forgotten. These are guys in whom I am very interested for a night's companionship or maybe more.

What I particularly enjoy about the guys who make no bones about staring is wondering about their opening gambit. Sometimes it's simply direct—a hand placed on a fairly neutral zone such as my knee but nonetheless a hand. Sometimes the hand gets there by a seeming accident as when the guy leans over to examine the view from my side window—"Look at that dairy farm!" Or he thinks he dropped something underneath my legs or whatever he can dream up to give his hand a reason to move accidentally but astutely. Long-forgotten high school moves suddenly surface. I give them a husky "Excuse me," which means they have to back off and try words. Since these are wordy men, they tend to have no problem launching into how they couldn't help but notice and how they couldn't help but act and how they meant no offense but Andrew Marvell said it hundreds of years ago and you and I know that poem. Sometimes I want to take my hands off the wheel and gave them a hand. I love how words have to brazen it out sometimes. I know, too, that guys talk to other guys. That's okay. I shoved my reputation in the path of an oncoming male long ago.

"And," my mother would enunciate like a television newscaster, "when are you ever going to marry one of these poets? I know what's going on. You don't think I know what's going on? Most of them are married already. You carry on with married men. But look, even your favorite poet, Anne What's-Her-Name, got married. You've told me her husband was good to her even if they did wind up getting divorced." My mother pauses strategically. "You have a good job. Why not a good husband, too?" Talking on the phone each week with a living parody is trying. Yet I have brought it on myself. I am a recusant.

Probing gets me nowhere. Like a Stalinist, she knows the party line and will repeat it until communism, which is to say matrimony, freezes over. I am left to reflect on long-term affairs conducted via airplanes connecting me for three years to Minneapolis and for four years to Chicago. It was hot and vital with both of them when we were together, but over time the miles made the heart grow colder. Ardor turned tumescent; I found myself in an airport lounge crying discreetly into a paper cup of cold coffee. I thought of leaving my job and with Mr. Minneapolis I offered to move there, but he kept putting me off until it became clear that the airport scene left him free for other assignations. Part of me said that was all right and part of me didn't. I consoled myself: I would meet another guy at another conference. I was made of something sturdier than pathos. If I was, in my mother's forthright words, "a fool," I was one of my own devising.

It has been passion I wanted more than love. Love congeals and thaws and congeals and thaws as the variable days between two people dictate. Love trickles down into affection, but passion can be fanned to keep flaming—until it goes dead out. No doubt the poems that are my totems are bad models. Each of us makes life into stories as if our lives were coherent tales with beginnings and endings, conveniently framed by birth and death. Anne's poems aren't like that. They are more like modulated outbursts. They are moments that have exploded. They are wrestling matches between irreconcilable feelings. They are no way to live (witness Anne's own life), but to me they seem the best way to live. I must be stubborn the way Bad Girls are stubborn. "Give that toy to your sister," my mother would command. Once I broke a toy in front of my mother's eyes. Hardly a heinous act but it brought down a string of Old Testament curses.

I sit in my apartment on a pleasant side street of a little college town that is replete with pleasant side streets. I suspect I will never live elsewhere than such an apartment with its books, two male calico cats, and comfortable mess. Perhaps I will retire to Europe where I will meet a tender, virile Italian poet who turns my head around completely. Anne liked fairy tales, too. Even as we debunk them, we need them for their spurious yet convincing magic. Lives should not be characterized by their narratives but by their allegiances. No one ever said that an allegiance to the truths in poems was an easy one. Those truths were not repeat-after-me creeds; they were complex and powerful emotions. To my mother I might as well be living in a phantasm.

It's late at night and there are no more halting yet often unexpectedly moving student poems to go over. They come from suburbs and cities and towns and farms and crossroads and Indian reservations but they want poetry, too. Going through the logical motions is not enough for them. I pick up Anne Sexton's book from 1966, *Live or Die*, and read for what may be the thousandth time "Menstruation at Forty":

> I was thinking of a son.
> The womb is not a clock
> nor a bell tolling,
> but in the eleventh month of its life
> I feel the November
> of the body as well as of the calendar.
> In two days it will be my birthday
> and as always the earth is done with its harvest.
> This time I hunt for death,
> the night I lean toward,

the night I want.
Well then—
speak of it!
It was in the womb all along.

I was thinking of a son...
You! The never acquired,
the never seeded or unfastened,
you of the genitals I feared,
the stalk and the puppy's breath.
Will I give you my eyes or his?
Will you be the David or the Susan?
(Those two names I picked and listened for.)
Can you be the man your fathers are—
the leg muscles from Michelangelo,
hands from Yugoslavia,
somewhere the peasant, Slavic and determined,
somewhere the survivor, bulging with life—
and could it still be possible,
all this with Susan's eyes?

All this without you—
two days gone in blood.
I myself will die without baptism,
a third daughter they didn't bother.
My death will come on my name day.
What's wrong with the name day?
It's only an angel of the sun.
Woman,
weaving a web over your own,
a thin and tangled poison.

Scorpio,
bad spider—
die!

My death from the wrists,
two name tags,
blood worn like a corsage
to bloom
one on the left and one on the right—
It's a warm room,
the place of the blood.
Leave the door open on its hinges!

Two days for your death
and two days until mine.

Love! That red disease—
year after year, David, you would make me wild!
David! Susan! David! David!
full and disheveled, hissing into the night,
never growing old,
waiting always for you on the porch…
year after year,
my carrot, my cabbage,
I would have possessed you before all women,
calling your name,
calling you mine.

Once, I asked my mother if she had wanted to have any more children. "What kind of question is that?" she asked me. Her tone had a quick edge of hurt that rarely entered her capable, matter-of-fact voice. I waited and she went on. "Well, we had two girls and we were thinking wouldn't it be nice to try again and maybe have a boy. But what if we had a girl? Having three girls—that's a lot of girls. I love you and your sister, you know that, but three girls is a lot of girls." She tried to laugh, but it came out as a thin, sharp sound. Although she was declaring her love, she wasn't looking directly at me. She was staring at the kitchen wall above my head where a calendar from Kimmelman's Dry Cleaners hung. "So we didn't." She picked up a pot from the dish drainer and began to dry it. My mother never bought an automatic dishwasher. She distrusted them.

"And did you have any regrets?" I asked, though I knew the answer beforehand.

"Regrets? Who has time for regrets?" For a second she looked at me directly—a deep, troubled second—and then turned away.

That was the end of the conversation.

As I sit with Anne's poem in the late-night stillness, I marvel at how she laid bare the most powerful of mixed feelings. For all her madness and darkness, in her best poems she was intensely honorable. That may seem a strange word, but I think it's the right one. She was terrifically hard on herself—too hard—but she spoke for those who are hard on themselves, particularly for women who are given enough social burdens to break the strongest back. Their bodies are part of those burdens and to say it shouldn't be so is to bring back the voice of my mother—"You have a woman's body." Shame was always not many steps from that body. It had more wretched faces than I could count.

For my mother my not having children is a genuine sadness. What is wrong with me? Am I really a woman? On the worst days she interrogates her own mothering, a self-laceration that ends in cold wrath. It's painful to witness; my protestations do no good. There are cruxes that do not get solved. Anne's fascination with suicide was far from wholesome but our American forgetting and ever moving on aren't wholesome either. Why live, if not to linger in the way poems can linger? Why not honor our confusions and vacillations as much as we honor our decisions? Why not feel how genuine regret can be? Why not say we have to live with our feelings however damaged they may be? Why not admit that we crave strong feeling even as it disrupts us? Why not accept how various the fullness of womanhood can be? Why not acknowledge poetry?

I sleep by myself, but in the morning mail there is a postcard of a beautiful Matisse painting from Gabe in Seattle. He is a twice-married and twice-divorced poet and he wants me to come and visit. The painting is of a woman in a green dress looking out a window. I think I will go.

Gregory Corso, b.1930

Like the kids I work with, Gregory Corso was a runaway. He didn't have a home to speak of; his mom, who was sixteen when she had him, went back to Italy and left him in New York City. He wound up in orphanages and foster homes. When his father remarried and took him in, he still kept running away. He got in trouble—petty theft. A kid named Amos once told me that stealing was the way to go: you get caught swiping a pair of jeans and get sent to the county jail where you are entitled to a bed, warm meals, and a roof over your head. It beat sleeping under a highway overpass.

There aren't many days when at some random moment—I'm filling out a referral form for services or reading a memo or regaling my otherwise empty automobile with lines from a favorite poem—I don't remember a particular kid and wonder what happened. The kid in this case—Amos—was an optimist, a born hustler always trying to turn a dime into a quarter. In the old days he would have been doing card tricks on the sidewalk and separating the credulous from their money. Where in "the dire miasma" (to quote Gregory) is Amos? He exited through a window of our so-called "haven" in the middle of the night—a runaway from the runaways.

Gregory Corso did some serious time—three years—beginning when he was seventeen. That's not very old to do time. He was brutalized in prison. Anyone who's thought twice about what happens in prisons knows what that means. He read a lot of books, too. He discovered the freedom of poetry while in jail. I want to write, "How ironic is that?" but I'm not sure about irony. There are too many strange corners where you can't tell the shadows from the lights. Irony is too easy. Gregory said about his jail time, "I left there [prison] a young man, educated in the ways of men at their worst and at their best. Sometimes, hell is a good place—if it proves to one that because it exists, so must its opposite, heaven exist." I have that quote on the door of my tiny office.

On many slow nights when I'm at the desk, which means I'm the intake person, the crisis worker, the shelter supervisor and the person who makes sure the toilets aren't plugged, I have read his poems. I know some of the short ones by heart—"On the Walls of a Dull Furnished Room" and "The Last Gangster" and "Birthplace Revisited" with its wonderful last line, "I pump him full of lost watches." Still, I like to read this or that poem and suck on it like a peppermint. I like carrying around a beat-up paperback that I bought back in the sixties. It's part of where I hail from and who I still am. I need to hold it in my hands and feel the paper—that yellowing fragility. Some of the kids have called me "Poet." They see the books and see me writing lines down on a pad every now and then. They don't know what that appellation (as the word-intoxicated Gregory might have put it) signifies but they know there is such a word. They like saying it as a name for someone. That's a start.

Around here anything is a start. I'm talking the abused, the neglected, and the rejected. I'm talking kids with parents who use, kids with parents doing ten to twenty, kids with parents who beat them, kids with a father who was murdered or a mother who overdosed. I'm talking a world that gets reported in the papers when something goes very wrong but that happens every unhappy day—kids strung out on meth, kids who are angrier than a Doberman on a short chain, kids who won't say a word, kids who do nothing but swear, kids who have been raped, burnt, bludgeoned. The statistic is that over a million kids run away every year in the United States. Some go to a friend's house and come home the next day. Lots don't.

Though I've worked with what they call "at-risk youth" for over twenty-five years, I haven't gotten used to the indifference, the matter-of-fact approach to what remains deeply distressing. I've never seen much salvation in the mountain of paperwork we do. It's well intentioned but it feels as though we use it to push the kids away, not to bring them close. Everyone is nervous about our liability but who is liable for the wages of human feeling? Impractical though the answer might sound, I would answer, "the poets." It's why I never wanted to rise in the social services chain of command. Though I believe in the old bumper sticker—Make Love, Not War—I'd go to some meeting and start throwing pencils and yelling because I'm one of those saps who feels we could do better. Like Gregory Corso's dear friend Jack Kerouac, I want to believe in America but when I think twice it seems that there really is no "our" to this country. "Our" is a notion that comes out every four years in some speeches and then crawls back into the hole of "my," as in "Don't locate that shelter for bad-news teenagers in 'my' neighborhood." The runaways I work with are throwaways and they know it. They aren't "our" children. Gregory refused to be a throwaway. For that alone he's a saint.

Poetry—as in a tattered paperback or my faulty memory—is about generosity. There's nothing that it is trying to hold onto, nothing that it unimpeachably owns. It's not trying to impress you, so you'll want to buy some. The opposite applies: it's trying to give itself away. It knows that one thing is always becoming another. Time doesn't stand still and though words seem to because they are particular, they, too, change, fade, and come back in new lives. Moving spirit is what everything has in common; you can't lasso it or hoard it. Corso once quipped to Kerouac that fish were "animalized water." Sounds ridiculous, a typical Corso-ism, but I don't think it is. Scientists know about stuff like anti-matter and quarks but we don't believe it. We see the big doings like people and buildings and fish and we love the visible there-ness, the beckoning solidity of them. "Look at that fish!" we holler. If we hollered, "Look at that animalized water!" it would be a very different world.

The kids who come to us—whether they knock on our door by themselves or are brought by a caseworker who needs to place them out of harm's way—are trying to survive. Typically they have been holding their breath for a long while. If they do something wrong at home—and it could be something completely harmless—they know hell could break loose. I've known kids who were hit for chewing too loudly, for not dusting the furniture, for going outside and looking at the sky. Sometimes they have been dealing with certifiable craziness on the part of parents, stepparents, guardians, or miscellaneous boyfriends or girlfriends who have moved into the house and become authority figures. More often they have been dealing with run-of-the-mill craziness, the frustrations, fears, and angers that are the unhappy core of too many lives. Most of them, too, are dealing with being poor. One trouble begets another.

I grew up in a trusting household. If my mom or dad said that we were going to Uncle Tony's on Sunday to have ice cream, it was as good as done. These are kids who have learned that the simplest declaration, such as "I'm going to make you a piece of toast," may not happen. The speaker may become distracted or forget or may not have meant it to begin with. Or it may be a minefield that can go off at any moment: "There's no fucking bread in this house! I told you to buy some! You steal my money!" When I talk to the kids, they often literally cock their head to the side and take a long view of whatever comes out of my mouth. When I say that they are old beyond their years, I mean that they have a wariness that comes from too much experience of too much instability at too early an age. People who wag their fingers at the oblivion of smack or a fifth of rum haven't lived with the corrosion of lies. Their sun comes up in the morning.

Generosity is not what runaways know nor is language as a presence in its own right. Everything they know is manipulated; everything is too tight or too loose: "I'm not giving you anything" or "Take what you want and leave me the hell alone." You can't win; that's why they wind up here. Though they often love the person who is making life hell, they can't go on. They may feel they are getting free or that they have given up on the one thing they knew. They may feel both at the same time. When a kid comes here, after the initial trepidation, there can be a typhoon of talk. All that dammed-up feeling breaks of itself. Like Gregory I'm your voluble Italian but I sit there and listen. Even if I only nod my head and say, "Yeah," it matters. They don't want anyone else's words; they need to find their own.

When the dam that was Gregory Corso broke, what came out were words in all their raw, fascinating, splendid beauty. Once I made a list of words that he used in his poems that you rarely, if ever, encountered in daily life. I found "verily," "credence," "alabaster," "promontory," "visage," "tocsin," "hoary" and "bereft" among others. He made up words, too, words like "autumnographer," "indoomable," "deatheme," "squawlark," "ingloomable," and "deathonic." I like the idea of making up words. That seems part of a poet's job—making up his or her own language. Poetry is primal; you have to feel the words' roots and how they can morph into new words. Gregory led a dodgy life, meaning he had trouble with drugs and where his next dollar was coming from, but he was at home in the soup pot of language. It was somewhere he could be even when he had no home. And it was one place—

to mix my metaphors—where he could shine like a million-watt, exuberant, General Poetics bulb. Like Edison, he was an inventor.

We deal with the immediate issues here. The kids need to be in a safe place; they need to be treating themselves and others in a healthy way; they need to see that there is something called "okay" and they can be that. We work to make those things happen but we also try to get them thinking about what they might want to do with their lives beyond the shelter. We ask them if they have any dreams. It's a hard question; life is what happens until it gets so bad that you run away. Life is what you are trying to avoid. When we ask them what they would like to be, they often stare hard as if to say, "What kind of social worker question is that? Don't you see what my life is like?"

When they do talk, they may say big, far-off dreams like NASCAR driver or movie star or more practical ones like nurse or car mechanic. No kid has ever said that he or she dreams of becoming a poet. Why would they? Poets aren't playing for a ball team or appearing in the Gregory Corso Show on primetime. In the career pamphlets that some guy from Human Services dumps here every six months, there's no mention of poets. Being a poet seems more like a calling than a vocation, more something you do because you have to do it. It's not the route to your own checking account or credit card or car payment. It's got nothing to do with the desires waiting for you at the local shopping mall. It resides in the words we use each day. As the likes of Amos would say, "No big thing."

Societies give their stamp to poets but don't necessarily want to recognize them in return. If the image flatters the society—the white-haired, wise yet scoffing Robert Frost—then it's okay. Frost was sharp enough and sly enough to give people what they thought they wanted and still be his own man. If, however, the image is of someone who likes the same sex or isn't very social or has hair all over the place and is prone to outbursts of spectacular and raunchy language, then the society is going to pass on that unpleasantness. If America can pass on Walt Whitman and Emily Dickinson, it certainly can pass on the ragamuffin iconoclast, mischievous humorist Gregory Corso.

Not that Gregory hungered for mainstream approval. His hunger was to remain human and he succeeded. Later in life when Allen Ginsberg had become a member of whatever establishment exists around poetry, a guy in a suit and tie, Gregory still ragged the poet as if it were 1956 and they were sitting in an all-night diner passing visions and cups of tea back and forth. Ginsberg was still "Ginzy."

Gregory Corso wasn't given poetry; he claimed it. Some part of him felt that he should be provided for by society because he was the authentic, shamanic item—a poet who arose from the urban cinders, a man without a birthright. Sometimes a kid who can't sleep will come into the front room where the desk is and hang out. We have a thousand rules at the shelter but my number-one rule is to be human. I want the kid who's sitting there on one of our dented folding chairs to feel, however cautiously, that's what both of us are. Most of what they know of being human is the brutal side. That's one reason for the ever-present book of poetry: "What's that? Who's that guy? Did he make that book? I never heard of him." They sound miffed. Fifteen-year-olds think they have heard of everyone.

Sometimes I read them a poem. Sometimes I ask them if they know the story of "The Poet," as I like to put it. "Which poet?" they ask me, "What do you mean 'The Poet'?" I tell them that though each poet has a different life, in being a poet each one lives the same story. Each one has to find the truest words. Each has to honor darkness and not fear happiness, even though it passes. Having heard their share of bullshit, they look at me with curiosity and skepticism. "Take this guy," I say and hold up one of Gregory's books. I talk about his early years, how he kept running away from one house after another, how he got in trouble with the law. As young Americans they think the world began four years ago. They can't believe someone who "lived a long time ago" was running away. "He really ran away? Lots? A guy who made a book ran away?" Sometimes they shake their heads, as if to say, "Can you believe it?"

A lot of exclaiming goes on in Corso poems, things like "My flesh is caught on the Inevitable Hook!" I like how he lets loose because there are many moments when I want to let loose, too, moments as when a kid is starting to feel that other people have had similar troubles long before he or she set foot on this earth. I want to exclaim, "Hola! The arrow of suffering comes after all of us! Look out! Take care of yourself!" I've been known to raise my voice. I tell them that the runaway Gregory Corso became a famous poet (as much as a poet can be famous in this country) and that he was one of the Beats.

"The who?" they ask me. "The what?" they ask me.

Their calm ignorance is one more wake-up call. If someone had told me thirty years ago I would be telling a kid with a buzz cut or shaved head or corn rows who the Beats were in a level, informative voice that sounds as though I'm explaining how the Eiffel Tower was constructed, I would have laughed out loud. I do tell them, however, beginning with the word "beatnik."

"What kind of word is that?" they shoot back at me. One kid observed, as if he were a linguistics professor, "That doesn't sound like an American word to me. That's a foreign word."

They do have the ears for language. Who knows how many lyrics they have memorized by rappers and rockers? I explain that it was mostly a put-down word used by the media who didn't like the idea of young people not getting with the program. They're listening to me when I say this because they have had troubles with the program themselves. When I ask them a question such as "What do you think of school?" I know I am going to get an earful. As a girl named Tori whose folder described her as "habitually truant" told me a few months ago, "If you have a different answer from the answer the teacher wants, then you don't have an answer. No one ever asks you, 'How you be thinking that? What kind of thinking you doing?' You know what I think? I think they don't want you to be thinking. They only want you to be answering."

I tell the kids that the Beats were poets who thought that America was a promise headed in the wrong direction. They thought that America was more interested in money than people. As poets they needed to put out some strong feelings to other people because they felt that they were muffled, as if over each of their heads there was a paper bag. They needed in the word of another Beat poet named Allen Ginsberg to "howl." This is news to the kids because most of them, despite their troubles and some bad habits they are developing, are true blue patriots. Some of them are stunned when they learn that the army doesn't want people who do drugs. "But I love America," they say. "I'd die for America." I believe them. They're fifteen, upset and haven't thought very far down the road.

I tell them that for these poets the word "beat" meant that they had had it, that they were not buying the official version. "It's like 'cool.' Do you know 'cool'?" I ask them in my Eiffel Tower voice. They nod because everyone knows "cool." It's a way to show something is good without getting excited and revealing your feelings. Even across the chasm of generations we can agree on "cool."

I ask them if they ever heard of Dwight Eisenhower—most haven't. Amos, as I recall, identified Ike as "a bald guy who won the war." Amos used to tell me that he respected knowledge more than anything. "We're on the same page, you and me, bro," he'd say in his smoothest, most sincere voice. When I asked Amos which war Ike had won, he told me, "What's it matter? You know—one of the wars. A big one." I didn't argue with him. "There's always some war goin' on," as a philosophical kid once told me. "War in your house, war in the streets, war with the Marines, war up your ass—what's the difference?"

Possessing as I do a sense of humor that can be traced back to *Mad Magazine*, I have a picture of Dwight and Mamie Eisenhower on a wall in my office and point to it as a visual aid during our beatnik discussion. "What do you think?" I ask them. It's quite the moment. I'm sitting there with a juvenile who has run away from a home where typically some horrendous things have happened and we're looking at this picture of beaming American wholesomeness (though I hear—what else is new?—that Mamie had trouble with the bottle). "That's quite the do she's got" is a typical comment. So is "Well, they seem like nice folks." Sometimes a black kid will venture that "They seem like awfully white folks. You know some white folks are whiter than other white folks are. Them's very white." It's said respectfully, like a reporter talking.

I tell them the Beat poets were upset with Eisenhower because he was such a boring, regular guy. They made fun of him for spending his time golfing and not looking too closely at anything that might trouble his routine. This puzzles the kids because a lot of them would like nothing better than two parents who were boring and regular, who didn't throw plates at them or shoot up drugs or start screaming for what seems like no reason. The golf course and mashed potatoes with gravy every night don't look so bad. Most tell me they would take their chances on the Eisenhowers. Amos said he would, though he couldn't see himself living in the White House. "Couldn't go to the bathroom in peace. Sure couldn't hide a *Penthouse* under your bed. Secret Service have your butt on the street fast."

This kind of two-in-the-morning talk goes nowhere special. As talk goes it resembles a poem where—because it's a poem—talk gets to have its way. That's sweet—the flow and spread and twitch of it—but it's tricky. It's not simply saying what's on your mind; it's imagining your mind, as when Gregory writes, "I should get married I should be good" in the poem "Marriage." Gregory is trying to figure out what he should do in that poem. He imagines a courtship, a wedding, "five running nose brats," "roaches and rats" in the apartment walls. He admits that he'll never get to marry Ingrid Bergman. He doesn't like the prospect of "Grocery store Blue Cross Gas & Electric Knights of Columbus." His words are like elves constructing and tearing down scenarios. His words are animalized; they have busy, impetuous lives—"Penguin dust, bring me penguin dust. I want penguin dust—." He sounds nuts; he makes sense, like talk at two-in-the-morning.

How those words in poems intermingle is mysterious. To anyone who wants *a* to equal *b* poetry is at a disadvantage because it never adds up right or computes or is equivalent. A poem is like a person—it doesn't have to exist and is fundamentally incomparable. The kids instinctively like that. They want there to be something beyond the tentacles of adult explanation. They want there to be some space that can't be taken away. The freedom behind Gregory's zaniness takes them aback. The poets in "Poets Hitchhiking on the

Highway" trade non sequiturs: "But the ocean chases / the fish" and "Suppose the / strawberry were / pushed into a mountain." The previously cited "penguin dust" speaks for its loony self. His playfulness surprises the kids. On the other side of their bleak knowledge there is some joy.

"Joy" is not a word in their vocabulary. They know anguish much better—the chafing of despondency and the inner shriek of terror. I tell them when I read them a poem by Gregory that they don't have to worry about whether they get it or not. This isn't a test. The last thing that Gregory is about is anxiety. He thought society was a conspiracy to produce anxiety. What I ask the various hair-twirling, foot-tapping young people in front of me to do is to listen. I know that there is joy—maybe furtive, maybe small, maybe confused, but joy, nonetheless—in listening to a poem. I know that no one reads to them. When, afterwards, I ask them something, it's more like "What kind of a guy do you think wrote this? Would you like to have met this guy? Can you see yourself writing something like this? Is this guy goofy or serious?" They love to have opinions; they love that someone will listen.

One of their favorites is called "Writ on the Eve of My 32nd Birthday." There's a note right underneath the poem in italics that it is "a slow thoughtful spontaneous poem." That note is very Corso, how he notes a tempo as if it were a piece of music and how he puts words together like "thoughtful" and "spontaneous." There's no reason that something spontaneous can't be thoughtful:

I am 32 years old
and finally I look my age, if not more.
Is it a good face what's no more a boy's face?
It seems fatter. And my hair,
it's stopped being curly. Is my nose big?
The lips are the same.
And the eyes, ah the eyes get better all the time.
32 and no wife, no baby; no baby hurts,
        but there's lots of time.

I don't act silly any more.
And because of it I have to hear from so-called friends:
"You've changed. You used to be so crazy so great."
They are not comfortable with me when I'm serious.
Let them go to the Radio City Music Hall.
32; saw all of Europe, met millions of people;
  was great for some, terrible for others.
I remember my 31st year when I cried:
"To think I may have to go another 31 years!"
I don't feel that way this birthday.
I feel I want to be wise with white hair in a tall library
  in a deep chair by a fireplace.
Another year in which I stole nothing.
8 years now and haven't stole a thing!
I stopped stealing!
But I still lie at times,
and still am shameless yet ashamed when it comes
  to asking for money.
32 years old and four hard real funny sad bad wonderful
  books of poetry
—the world owes me a million dollars.
I think I had a pretty weird 32 years.
And it weren't up to me, none of it.
No choice of two roads; if there were,
  I don't doubt I'd have chosen both.
I like to think *chance* had it I play the bell.
The clue, perhaps, is in my unabashed declaration:
"I'm good example there's such a thing as called soul."
I love poetry because it makes me love
  and presents me life.
And of all the fires that die in me,
there's one burns like the sun;

it might not make day my personal life,
my association with people,
or my behavior toward society,
but it does tell me my soul has a shadow.

That's a lot to take in; I ask them if they'd like to hear it again. Most times they want to and they ask me what a word means such as "unabashed." The poem interests them because thirty-two years old is an eternity. "That's old," as more than one fifteen-year-old has said. Then the kid looks over at me with my gray ponytail and gray stubble of a beard and realizes I'm even older than that, maybe something unthinkable like fifty-five or sixty. Sometimes a kid will give a little smile as if to say, "No hard feelings, geezer."

For them to imagine themselves as being thirty-two some day is Oz. They aren't on the success path, the what-good-things-is-life-going-to-give-me path. They're on the survival path, which too many times turns out to be the self-destruction path. To them thirty-two means you have pretty much lost out on life. There couldn't be much fun left in you when you're thirty-two. The fractured intensity of coping has left a lot of them with tired hearts.

I ask them if they've been through changes—the way that Gregory says people tell him that he's changed. I ask them what they were like when they were around eleven and what they are like now. They get reflective. No one asks them a question like that, and if they are willing, which they aren't always, they start talking about how they were still a kid back then. Sometimes they get wistful; sometimes they get amused. Sometimes it's too dark back there.

I ask them if Gregory Corso seems honest to them. To a kid, they say that he does: he doesn't only say good things about himself—that's being honest. They're impressed that he talks about things like stealing and being ashamed. They like that he calls his life "weird." They like that he wants to have a baby—not only the girls like that but most of the guys, too. They like the attitude that goes with his writing that life owed him "a million dollars." More than one kid has told me that Gregory Corso seems like "a real person." That's a big compliment. Gregory's dead now; I should have written him a letter when he was alive and told him the good things some runaways in south Florida said about him.

I ask them if they ever have written a poem—a lot have. They may be flunking out of school but they write what they call poems. What has touched me to the quick is that a kid will have written poetry not just because he or she senses that poetry is a way to confront the various hells but to find a way through them. They sense the tie between poetry and courage. To someone who endlessly has been told to "shut up," poetry is an undeniable language. Somewhere inside them they know that.

Sometimes I ask if maybe they'd like to write a poem like Corso's but from their own age. I tell them they can say what they want. I tell them that I'd like to see it if they do it but they don't have to do it. I'm not a teacher and poetry isn't a chore like making your bed or cleaning up after yourself. I remember how one night I read Gregory's poem to a girl named Taffy who had been in the shelter for two days. She gave me this poem the next morning. She had a whole journal of poems with her in her backpack. She also had an ugly bruise on her face and cuts on her arms—a mutilator.

Written on the Eve of My 16th Birthday

How did I get here?
Where to begin?
I haven't given up jump rope yet—
"A" my name is Alice
And my husband's name is Al
We come from Alaska..."
My name isn't Alice but that doesn't matter.
I haven't given up sitting on a swing
In the schoolyard and pushing myself up
Into the sky that doesn't want me.
I must still be a child—
A child who has a stepfather who

Crawls into bed and touches her everywhere
And tells her she will die
If she makes a sound.
I must still be a child
Waiting for Santa Claus
Waiting for my mother to confront my stepfather.
SHE KNEW!!!!
I must be all grown up.
Is this all I get?
A skinny bed in a shelter
Mac with icky cheese on a Styrofoam plate
A pair of sneakers I wouldn't give to a nun.
I want a boyfriend who
Wants more from me than sex.
I want a room that has no locks
Because I'm not afraid.
I must still be a child
Because when night comes I get afraid
And because I wrote a poem and feel better.

I keep that poem on my desk so I can read it whenever I need to read it, which is often. I remind myself that a fifteen-year-old wrote that and that I better remember with whom I am dealing each day. I am not dealing with half people, as the word "teenager" implies; I am dealing with people who already know a great deal. Poetry is like lightning. It strikes when it strikes and it doesn't care about things such as where you went to school or how old you are. It wants to make our souls jump.

Taffy and I have stayed in touch. She's in her mid-twenties, has had some miserable relationships with some miserable guys, dropped out of the local community college a couple times, and works at a big box store where she wears what she calls "the world's ugliest apron." That doesn't sound like much but then Gregory Corso's life doesn't sound like the stuff of *Who's Who in America*. Her big achievement is that she doesn't cut herself. She doesn't hate herself or blame herself for what other people have done to her. I'm proud of her for that.

We meet for coffee and talk about life in the shelter and poetry. She still fills up notebooks with poems. I've encouraged her to publish but she's not interested. The notion of a literary journal that emanates from some faraway university is unreal to her. She read once at a local open mic but didn't like it. She's shy. And what does that stuff matter? That's my stuff not hers. Her poems are her oxygen. They may take her into other people's lives and they may not. Poetry was a medium before there were media.

It's hard in what-have-you-done-for-me-lately, get-ahead America to grasp how something that doesn't seem to matter at all could matter the most. Look at the example of the man to whom Allen Ginsberg dedicated his *Selected Poems*. The inscription reads, "To Gregorio Nunzio Corso, Wisdom Maestro, American Genius of Antique and Modern Idiom, Father Poet of Concision." Gregory, a natural, penniless loser, turned himself upside down and prankster-like refused a long face. He dove so deeply into his fate that he came out the other side. He showed how a poet in the United States must be a freelance spirit. There aren't guilds or tribes or hoards of legends and myths to preserve and pass on. There are just a bunch of individuals pushing their lives wherever they push them. Everyone has a shopping cart full of intentions. Everyone is trying to pull pleasure off the shelf and get a bargain at the same time. Along comes Gregory Corso who stole what he could get his hands on—candy bars and poetry were there for the taking. As Amos noted, if you want to be recognized the first thing is to take something that is not yours. Don't sulk—steal.

Poetry isn't on the thoughtless pleasure shelf or on the material goods shelf. Poetry is more like a wrapper lying in the aisle or a cloud floating by. It's unofficial. Whenever it's official, it's sentimental at best and self-righteous at worst. That's why I love Gregory Corso. He couldn't have been official if he wanted to. Belief tends to own people; Gregory liked being free. He was the jester in his own life, the antic anti-Buddha Buddha, but he was terrifically serious, too. He knew we only come through as Amos or Gregory or Taffy one time and one time only. He knew that poetry helps us recognize that better than anything because a real poem is a fingerprint—it's that distinct. The words are actual as breath, like the wheeze at night of my grandmother Rosa when I was a little boy.

"My life's kind of crummy," Taffy told me the last time I saw her, "but I'm okay with it." She paused. "I don't know if that's good or bad. What I really like to do is write poems. No one is going to pay me to do that. So...." After a small sigh, she went on. "I'm thinking of going to cosmetology school. I like hair almost as much as I like poetry. I bet you noticed that I'm letting mine grow." She smiled. I quoted Gregory's line, "And my hair, / it's stopped being curly." She told me that she remembered that line.

"You were the first person I met who was open about poetry." She said this quietly, looking only partially at me and kneading the rim of a paper cup with both hands. "I was what they call FUBB—'Fucked Up Beyond Belief.' I get that now. I can even joke about it with the girls in the store. You know, like 'I used to be crazy but, hey, I knew where the 'on' switch was.' That's more than a lot of people know who are buying table saws. But when I think back to what I was, when I see myself back then, it creeps me out. I could have died pretty easy."

It's hard for things to not get soggy between us. She's got a real heart and a real history. I'm not sure how that heart is going to fare in this world. I've been up and down myself—as in two divorces. When we get to one of these fraught moments, when we know we need to lighten up, I'll blurt one of Gregory's non sequiturs:

"Firestoves! Gas! Couch!"

Taffy beams. "Thunder! Dinosaurs! Midgets!"

"Cauliflower! Moolah! Intestines!"

"Chalk! Laser Beams! Barbecue!"

We can do this foolishness for many minutes. We can interrupt the remainder of our conversation whenever we feel like it. We can leave each other with a whole string of them: "Goodbye! Dogbody! Ambulance! Sonata!

Chlorine! Goodbye!" Sometimes I sense people staring at us: whatever are that scraggly pony tail, big nose guy and that young woman with extra eye shadow doing? It's like a nutty verbal chess game. Or it's not like anything. It's pure Gregory-ness let loose in the world. It's the play we talk about but don't do. It exhilarates us to the point where we can't stop smiling.

I keep telling the kids at the shelter stories about poets. There are such people, I tell them. I've even known some in my own life. I tell them that I've known poets who ran away to this shelter. They look at me blankly. Or maybe there's a glimmer in their eyes. Maybe there is something over the next hill that isn't like what has happened before. Maybe it lies in something as common as words—"my soul has a shadow."

When I talk to them, I don't try to brush away the pain in Gregory's life. I tell them he scuffled. How else could it be? He wanted to be a poet full time and he was a poet full time. He wasn't a hyphen—a poet-professor or a poet-doctor or a poet-insurance-executive. He was a poet, pure and simple. That seems impossible but he did it. And he never went back to jail. From what I know of him he could be plenty difficult but he had a dignity, too. He got to live the life. Whenever we are with poetry—"almost profound," to quote Gregory—we get to live the life. "Firestoves! Gas! Couch!"

Sylvia Plath, b.1932

"Waitress." The woman actually knocks on the side of her drinking glass with a knife to demonstrate that she is trying to get my attention. "Oh, waitress," she burbles. She has a high, fruity voice of which she seems proud for some demented reason. I can see her calling some local women's club to order by knocking on the side of a glass while beaming a self-satisfied smile. I don't dwell on that, though, because I've seen worse. People jump up and down; people throw pennies; people yodel. I'm used to these ways in which grown-ups act like children—except children are more polite to an adult stranger like myself.

I'm used to being addressed generically. That's more okay with me than not. I don't like places where you introduce yourself with "Hi, I'm Suzie Creamcheese and I'm your server tonight." What kind of introduction is that? If you're going to do it, then do it: "Hi, I'm Cathy. I'm your server tonight. I had my first crush at the age of eleven on Hank Seymour who preferred his baseball card collection to my company. I got my period a year later during geography class and ran out of the room shrieking. Everyone laughed at me. The next week our teacher Miss Halstead was fired for drinking on the job and everyone forgot about my period."

At Mickey's Burger Pub, we wear plastic nametags. Some people read them and then immediately forget. Some people never really look at you. Some people can't read. You'd be surprised at how many people can't read or read very poorly. I've thought of having the owner, whose name is Joe (he didn't want to change the sign when he bought the place), print out a tag that reads "Waitress." Then I could be Waitress Cathy, distant cousin to the famous doll, Chatty Cathy.

Sylvia Plath waited tables one summer. She got sick, though, and went home and never returned. I'm sure she worked hard at it because she worked hard at everything, an eager beaver—or a driven beaver; I'm not sure which. I can imagine her bustling around while plotting a story for the likes of *Mademoiselle* in what more than one guy must have told her was a very pretty head. She didn't come from money, so she knew what a dollar was. When you waitress, you learn what a dollar is because you handle a lot of them. Life is a buck fifty. Your apron gets filled with dollars and quarters. At the end of your shift it feels like a lot of money but isn't. There's part of me that thinks those dollar bills are going to be tens and twenties. That must be the poet in me.

I'm not sure Sylvia had the personality for this line of work. You need to be amiable up to a point. Past that point you have to shut people and their stupidity out. That can be hard for a woman to do. We're brought up to act as though it isn't really stupidity—vagueness maybe or a touch of bad manners but not out and out stupidity. Sylvia knew how cretinous that pretending was but like most women she had a hard time shaking it. Beyond the balancing act of being friendly and distant at the same time, the need for a comfortable, no-nonsense pair of shoes outweighs any *Mademoiselle* fantasy. Shoes, of course, matter to women because shoes, unlike the typical pair of feet in them, can be beautiful. I wear these walking shoes at work that are good for my feet but ugly—not much different from what the lady tapping on the water glass is wearing. Once in a long while, I splurge on a pair of designer knock-offs that gather dust in the closet. I like looking in the closet, though. Being "sensible," as in "You need a pair of sensible shoes," is hard. There's more fun in being insensible.

Sylvia was pretty big on the fantasy-of-glamour angle and must have had her share of shoes. That sort of bugs me when I read about her, that the biographers go into all this psychological stuff about her father's death and her trauma but they don't spend any time on Sylvia's shopping. How can you know a woman when you have no sense of how she shopped? It's a serious oversight. Sylvia wrote for girl's magazines and then for women's magazines and that tremor of glamour, that glint of romance, is something most women need. Women aren't stolid. We aren't wired up like that. The question is, where do you go to get your glamour fix? Maybe reading an article or a story (back in the old days) or seeing a film does it for you and you get by in life by lifting your horizon vicariously. Or maybe it doesn't. Maybe you have to dress up and throw yourself back at some hunk of a British poet when he throws himself at you. Maybe you even take a bite out of him. You can imagine Sylvia writing one of those "Notes" or "Hints" female publications are so fond of: "A little savagery can do wonders for romance."

Being a waitress has been a blessing to me while I try to figure out what I'm doing with my quarter-of-a-century-long life. It's probably been a good thing that I have to deal with people like Mrs. Country-Club-Chairwoman-Having-a-Bad-Hair-Day who bangs on the side of her glass so she can receive an extra serving of ranch dressing. When I look down at her bowl, the salad—ancient iceberg lettuce gussied up with a few carrot shavings, a mummified cherry tomato, and a dehydrated cucumber slice—looks fairly drenched already. I smile, however, a good-egg smile that I've been conditioned to put on since the age of three, and fetch another packet of chemical sludge. I should tell her this stuff is probably clogging her arteries and has a million calories but you have to let people make their own choices. When I'm asked for recommendations, I stick with the burgers. You get better tips if you tell people what they want to hear in the first place.

I waitressed at Mickey's through my two years of graduate school. I didn't have a fellowship or a scholarship. I wasn't poor enough or brilliant enough. The poems that earned me a Master of Fine Arts degree were "interesting"—an always deadly and dismissive word used by a visiting poet—but not set-the-world-on-fire fantastic. Sylvia Plath, on the other hand, got a free ride to Cambridge, England. That's how her life worked. You never envy her, though, because she was Sylvia Plath. You think about the writing she did and you quiver with amazement and fear. She was the princess who was also the frog except everyone didn't know about the frog part until they read her poems. I could buy an airline ticket to England and visit her often desecrated grave but I haven't yet. I'm out here in the Midwest where the view goes on forever but there's not much to see. I have to say that I've gotten to like silos, the quiet geometry of them, but I've gotten to like the local beer, too. That's not a particularly good sign. I can't imagine Sylvia seated in one of the booths at Mickey's sharing a pitcher of brew and munching stale corn chips with some backward baseball caps and state university tee shirts. I can't imagine her sitting and listening to conversations in which every other word is "like," as in "I like had a car but like it broke like." She was fearlessly and thoroughly articulate. She had class.

I could get up in the morning and put on some sign of class and glamour such as the string of pearls my parents gave me when I turned sixteen. I'm not sure where I would go with them. It wouldn't fit in at Mickey's. It wouldn't fit in at the Laundromat. It wouldn't fit in at the Tarantula Café, which is my hangout—latte and reggae. I like the idea, however. I like it a lot. I'm weary of grunge. Though I don't have much of it, and what I do have I work hard for, it's not money I want. I want occasions that have some class to them. I've been dressing down my whole life; it's put me in the emotional basement. I've been casual for too long. I think that's why I've broken up with three guys in the past year. Granted, not one of them was Ted Hughes, but they were in the acceptable zone. It's been too casual, though: "Hi." "Hi." "Wanna fuck?" "Sure. Why not?" I exaggerate but not a great deal. And there have been some good fucks in there. Still, there's been a lot missing—like class.

I like those old black and white movies with women like Katherine Hepburn and guys like Cary Grant where a breeze of svelte manners caresses each feeling: little endearments, little polite gestures, little compliments, little rhetorical questions, little silly jokes, even little fusses and spats. Straight-up sex isn't enough, though for Plath's generation the charm must have hardened and they needed sex to explode it. Sylvia wanted to get it on the way any healthy woman wants to get it on, but she was tied up in worry knots. "Do I dare?" seems more a woman's line than a man's. As a waitress in a Midwestern college town, I'm at the perfunctory end of the rainbow. I don't fantasize about sex; I fantasize about the polite murmur that makes sex civilized. I fantasize about winks and double entendres. That excites me. I want to linger.

Sylvia craved class but mocked it too—how quickly it can turn into dowdiness. That smart ambivalence is a big part of her equation, glamour and realism duking it out in her soul. When I first started reading her poems, I thought, "Why is she doing this? What is this formality about? Why the fuss and bother? What is she trying to prove?" I was a typical American high school kid who knew as much about poetry as a squirrel does. I think we got as far as Poe in my American literature class. Even Frost seemed too scarily modern for our teacher, Mr. Boddicker, whose idea of a great book was *The Last of the Mohicans*. I went out on my own and read some Ferlinghetti and Ginsberg and then when I read Plath I thought, "What's with her? How come she isn't cool? What's her hang up?"

It wasn't a hang up, though, was it? It was art. You could have fooled me. I can see myself (it's not that long ago this happened as much as it feels like centuries) sitting with Plath's first book in my hands. Marcie Kaplan, who wore baggy turtlenecks and preferred tequila to grass and beer, told me I had to read Sylvia Plath, but that I should start at the beginning "to get the real effect and understand her journey." Marcie loved the word "journey." She was a year ahead of me and told me the most thrilling taste in the world was sperm. Since I was still pretty keen on grape popsicles, I looked up to her. She was the editor of our high school literary magazine, *The Trident*. After school you could hear her breathlessly emoting a poem by Plath or Dylan Thomas or T. S. Eliot through the closed door of the magazine's tiny office. She was affected but she wasn't a phony.

At table six Mrs. Country Club is happy as a clam at high tide with her extra portion of ranch dressing. She's won a round in the endless struggle of self-assertion. I smile graciously and ask her if I can get anything else. "Not right now," she says pointedly. She wants it known that I'm on call. She's the type who puts you through your paces, then leaves you a stingy tip because you didn't put enough ice in the ice water—or too much ice. I walk into the back area where my bag is and my copy of *Ariel* that I carry around as a totem, source of equivocal solace, and dire companion. *Ariel*, of course, is the second book. The first book contains the poems from the late fifties that Marcie was keen on, *The Colossus and Other Poems*.

I have to give Marcie credit. Because it all happened so suddenly with Plath—I mean "Bang! Here are some genius poems and I'm out of here"—you do well to take your time. In terms of poetry, her little life was a big life. I spent a lot of time in my bedroom heeding Marcie's advice and reading Book Number One. I can't say exactly why I was enthralled. I didn't understand Plath in the sense of explicating her but that wasn't what it was about anyway. "Understanding" was something you did in classrooms that put you to sleep—formulaic words you wrote to receive a grade and to silence poetry. Plath's poetry was more like a drug concocted from language. I felt like someone stumbling into a séance but not knowing whose spirit was being raised. It was eerie. I knew that she had killed herself. It must have been the first thing Marcie told me about Sylvia Plath. Sensitive high school students love the notion of suicide-as-revenge. It's not only the world that fucks you up; you can fuck yourself up. That's a wretched consolation but I was there, too.

I used to pace back and forth between my bureau and my bed speaking the poems out loud. Marcie was right again with that one. You had to say them aloud to get the magic. Looking at them on the page was like looking at bacteria under a microscope—those things couldn't hurt you, not unless, of course, you had them in your body. I wanted Plath's poetry in my body. Saying it to the silent walls was how I ingested it. Saying it broke a silence inside me. Her poetry was a sort of wheedling hurt, though a hurt I needed. If that sounds bleak, I can only plead self-knowledge. The way that poetry helps you isn't the keep-smiling, uplift way. It's the way that leads through the chasms in people and can be frightening. Sylvia Plath didn't lead me down Death Street; she didn't bring me back either. She did show me that she, another young woman in another time, had been there and done more than take notes.

All this intensity about some words in a slim book means that you keep poetry to yourself. If you're lucky you meet some other people like Marcie who also like poetry—which is rare because most people don't. You don't walk up to Mrs. Country-Club-with-the-Bad-Dye-Job and ask her if, by the way, she's read any Sylvia Plath lately. How about a little Plath as an appetizer? Doesn't go down easy. Sticks in your craw and may make you gag on existence. Anxious hives and nightmares can be side effects. Better off staying with the mozzarella sticks.

When I get back to my demanding diner, she has an addled look of surfeit on her face. There's nothing like eating too much to soothe a person, though she's fretting to her companion, a thin, muscled woman who must have a wicked forehand, about calories. I smile ironically and ask if they would like dessert but she goes on fretting. I wait for some seconds and say that I'll give them more time to ponder—there's no hurry. She's on a bender about her weight—"five extra pounds"—and still doesn't acknowledge me. I walk off. Mrs. Getting-a-Big-Tummy doesn't look up.

Sylvia wrote, "My hours are married to shadow," and sometimes I feel like that shadow. What that line says to me, which is from the title poem of Book Number One, is that even when you're here you're not here. I'm walking around for six hours at Mickey's serving people food, but I'm a role, not a person. I'm doing a job. Somewhere inside that job of making sure the squeezable ketchup containers get refilled and chatting with the regulars and adding up the bill on her pocket calculator is this person Cathy who writes poems about a boyfriend who wanted to be called by the name of his car—Camaro—or about the time she accidentally drove a sewing needle through a finger tip in home economics class. Cathy knows that writing these poems is no way to make a living but isn't real interested in making a big-time living because she likes to write poems. Part of Cathy is good with being a role and hiding out and part of her isn't happy at all because she loses track of herself. She doesn't have to marry it—she becomes the Shadow.

What's troubling me is whether I'm always in a role, whether all I can do is go through the motions because the motions define you to other people. The motions are all other people really want to know about you. A waitress waits on people; a student studies; a poet writes poems—but what sort of poems? Maybe that sounds like adolescent existentialism but I haven't been able to shake it. I think that's part of all the father stuff Sylvia Plath wrote about. You have this person in your life from the other sex and that person is supposed to mean a lot to you. So you're the Daughter but the Daughter tends to be a Shadow because she isn't the Son. It's literally that in my case because I have a brother who was a big-deal athlete in high school. He's not a bad guy at all. He's pretty modest in fact. Still, he was the Son and I was the lowercase daughter.

My dad is an agreeable, easy-going guy, the kind who walks around and whistles Perry Como songs from the fifties that are limp but pleasant. He's a civil engineer. Roads are what turn him on; asphalt is his poetry. He isn't by any stretch of any imagination the Germanic type Plath writes about in poems such as "Daddy" that sound angry and hysterical to a lot of people, where she's writing that "Every woman adores a Fascist." Whew! What a line! Sylvia was one barbed wire. But I think that's the point. Even on a good day too much goes unsaid; too much gets buried. When it finally gets said, it needs to explode. It's emotional shrapnel. Even if your dad isn't a Nazi, it needs to explode. I know that being a man is unbearable; that's why there are wars. But being a woman is unbearable, too, like setting a table during an earthquake.

Think about it, this woman getting scholarships and winning prizes and getting good grades and being real ambitious to be the best at whatever she's doing and inside she's a fierce, quivering wreck. When she tries to kill herself or she's depressed, she has to talk to people about this wreck. They listen to her or they do more extreme things that frighten me intensely such as shoot electricity through her head, but she's still Sylvia who's "married"—she would use that verb of all the verbs in the world—to the shadows of her tumultuous feelings. The experts try to make her feel better about herself but it's not like they're changing the world to make it easier for Sylvia to live because how could they? They're people doing their jobs, playing their roles. They're serving up mental health instead of hamburgers and Sylvia's taking it in the way she sat in the malt shop near Smith College sipping a shake with her burger. She's trying to be substantial, a thing of Substance that you could see smiling and looking pretty on a magazine cover. She's not trying to be a Shadow, but the Shadow doesn't go away.

Neither has the Dessert-Pondering-Woman who waves me over with a fake, friendly smile and asks me what the blueberry pie is like. I'm not about to tell her that our desserts come to us frozen from who knows where and all we do is microwave the stuff ("Nuke it!"), so I tell her our blueberry pie is "especially delicious." I'm a poet—I can't resist words. I arch my pierced eyebrows as if to say, "Would I lie to you, honey?" Of course, her question is more like a statement. She needs a scintilla of waitress confirmation to go ahead and do what she already has her mind and stomach set on. It's a dance step I do every working day. Tell 'em what they want to hear.

Lying feels good. Women tend to be fools for sincerity. When I lie like that—and for all I know she'll love the pie—it puts me in touch with that part of Sylvia that is artfully, and at times boisterously, bad mannered—"there's a stink of fat and baby crap," as she forthrightly put it. Sylvia was a poet and poets are people who obey the truth of their feelings. They aren't newspaper reporters or scientists; they make stuff up to confirm the fire in their pulses. They know that what we call "life" is made up to begin with so we might as well enjoy it. It's not easy for people, particularly out here in Pickup Truck Land, to get their minds around that one. They tend to go for the Gospel truth—whether biblical, automotive, political—they're interchangeable. Feigning imaginations need not apply. You don't see poets reading when Republican presidents get inaugurated. It would be an insult to their literal-minded constituency. I'm not a snob to say that I can see why Sylvia wound up in England.

Maybe on a bad night the good folk who are blessed by God have a premonition that there's something like Sylvia Plath out there, something that groans and screams and throws exclamation marks around like fervent confetti. Maybe they sense there's trouble out there that they would just as soon not know about. Maybe they sense that poetry is a kind of corruption because it won't leave words alone. Maybe they fear poetry because it doesn't talk straight, because it insists that metaphor dwells inside of everything, that feeling can be pushed aside but never goes away. Sylvia's wise-ass, hyperbolic tone—"is it ugly, is it beautiful"—is not going to reassure anyone, unless you find over-the-top to be comforting. I do. Since life is crazy, let's see what it's about.

If you grow up in America and you take in the swill of the advertising, political posturing, and endless sit-com-cop-show-cartoon jabbering—one long, moronic placebo—then you feel a certain joy in shredding a few pounds of shrink-wrapped crap. Twenty years later, Sylvia might have been on

Saturday Night Live but I'm glad that didn't happen. That stuff disappears. It makes you laugh and you might tell someone else how it made you laugh but then you forget it. Sylvia Plath is unforgettable because she was an artist who could be angry and amused at the same time. She was an artist who for a time walked the difficult line of admitting the world's harm and ministering to it in her poems. She was an artist who clung to her words like so many brick life preservers. And she was willing to go down with them.

Listen to how her poems get going. This is the beginning of "The Applicant":

First, are you our sort of a person?
Do you wear
A glass eye, false teeth or a crutch,
A brace or a hook,
Rubber breasts or a rubber crotch,

Stitches to show something's missing? No, no? Then
How can we give you a thing?
Stop crying.
Open your hand.
Empty? Empty. Here is a hand

To fill it and willing
To bring teacups and roll away headaches
And do whatever you tell it.
Will you marry it?

This sounds like standup but it's fiercer. It comes from the same place that an outlaw writer like William S. Burroughs comes from—a refusal to ignore how insensate people can be and an almost wanton delight in pointing it out. It's more than satire; it's what they used to call "gallows humor." For a man it's okay to do this—men being the brutes who walk on the battlefields and crack jokes about the corpses—but for a woman to be so frank is verboten. Sylvia habitually crossed big boundaries. I wonder if she got scared or looked back or pined for something easier that would demand less of her. I doubt it, though. She wanted to ride wherever poetry took her.

Then there is the opening of "Lesbos":

> Viciousness in the kitchen!
> The potatoes hiss.
> It is all Hollywood, windowless,
> The fluorescent light wincing on and off like a terrible migraine,
> Coy paper strips for doors—
> Stage curtains, a widow's frizz.
> And I, love, am a pathological liar,
> And my child—look at her, face down on the floor,
> Little unstrung puppet, kicking to disappear—

It would be a rare writing teacher who would tell you to begin a poem with an exclamation mark. It's like betting all your money on your first poker hand. "Wait," the voice of reason would say, "see what happens;" but there was no waiting for Peremptory Sylvia. When I look back I can see I shouldn't have been surprised that the instructor in my undergrad poetry survey course spent two wary days circling Sylvia and then moved on. You might have thought she had been dropped into the middle of war-torn Bosnia—paramilitary forces on all sides of her, mines beneath her, planes strafing. All she had to cover herself with was *The Norton Anthology*. She explained Plath to us as not so much a poet as a sort of historical emblem, the pre-feminist shriek that led to better days. Men had done bad things to her, but she managed to write some poems about it before sticking her head in the oven. The poems were more than a little weird but we could forgive her. The instructor confessed at the end that she didn't much like Sylvia Plath. She found her "shrill."

I went up after the second lecture and asked her if she thought Sylvia Plath was a person. She looked balefully at me, a look reserved for undergraduate dullards, and answered in her cultivated, slightly nasal voice that, of course, she thought Plath was a person. I asked her why then didn't she treat Plath as a person—someone who wrote for *Mademoiselle* and wanted to be a mom and had terrible depressions and strove to please and told jokes and liked England and on and on. "Yes," she said, "Plath was a person. Thank you for reminding me." She smiled a kind, dismissive, ironic smile. I should have quoted from "Magi," a poem that wasn't in the mammoth anthology: "The abstracts hover like dull angels..."

It bothers me because this Sylvia who worried about whether her skirt and blouse matched and who made recipes out of *The Joy of Cooking* was a world-class subversive. The relentless thrust of Sylvia's life and art is that she didn't want to be recruited into any army of right-thinking people. She hated armies of right-thinking people. If there is a great protest poet it is Sylvia: her poetry protests the bludgeoning we undergo to achieve our sad identities. Like so much folded and pressed laundry she brings the attitudes of the brisk, we-know-what-we-are-doing world right into the poems. Those know-it-alls who can remove the soul's spots are her hellhounds, the smiling, persuading faces that turn one thing into another and never let anything be. They are the experts the newspapers are forever citing who invariably know better. Look at what they did to her! Shot her full of electricity, praised her, felt sorry for her, put her in headlines when she tried to kill herself with their pills ("Local girl missing"), made a celebrity of sorts of her, abandoned her, then canonized her. "Now your head, excuse me, is empty," the voice in "The Applicant" says. Sylvia knew that voice with a vengeance. She mocked it because she felt it so acutely. She knew what century she was living in, the one that made people disposable on a previously unbelievable scale. Isn't disposability what the twentieth century has taught? Someone else will carry the banners or do the corporate job or drive the car into the traffic jam or buy the new, better machine or spout the ideology. You aren't necessary; you aren't unique; you're a unit. Keep your messy, individual feelings to yourself, please.

What if this sane world is peopled with monsters? What if Mrs. Blue Teeth, who has finished her gooey pie and is gesticulating again in my direction, is a monster of sorts? What if myths are real and Medusa and Perseus and Gulliver and Midas are all right here right now and not in some book or never-never land? What if the depth of human feeling at any given moment is legendary yet nonetheless silly, nonetheless petty, nonetheless like Mrs. Blue Teeth who wants to know if she can have more iced coffee or whether she will have to pay for a refill. It's a big issue but I'm the Angel of Refills and tell her the iced coffee is on the house, all the mother fucking, cock teasing, cunt lapping iced coffee she can drink. I don't say those adjectives, though. I just go and get more iced coffee.

I think Plath intuited that every moment of our experience on earth is mythic, that inside each name is an animal that shouts to be let out. She never lapses into anecdote; she never tells a story to tell a story. She is always going into the dream world that is the deeper, real world. She feels how unrelentingly strange the whole experience of being alive is. She welcomes it. Where did that poem "The Colossus" come from? What is the creature she writes about? I don't know:

Nights, I squat in the cornucopia
Of your left ear, out of the wind,

Counting the red stars and those of plum-color.
The sun rises under the pillar of your tongue.
My hours are married to shadow.

I keep coming back to that last line. It's my unhappy but necessary charm. For a time when I was a senior in high school I was where Sylvia was—upset and lost enough to kill myself. Clinically, I was "depressed," a word that hides a harrowing world. I, too, took pills. I didn't crawl under a porch, though, and wait to die. I locked my bedroom door. I remember seeming to wake to the sound of the door splintering as a neighbor put an axe to it and thinking, "What is that sound? I have never heard that sound before. Is this what it's like to be dead? You hear sounds you have never heard before?"

Then I was unconscious again. Then I was taken to the hospital and had my stomach pumped. Then I lived. But I still hear that sound—wood screaming.

If you sojourn in the world of the dead, you must see life differently. You must feel how everything we denominate with language is something impossibly large, much larger than our word-spewing minds. I think that's what the Colossus is—the hugeness of any experience, how any aspect of being is driven by energy that is super-atomic. In that sense, any noun can be capitalized—Hospital, for instance. You think of the strangeness of a hospital—the corridors, the machines, the nurses in white, the big beds, the sterility of the implements, and it seems like a vision because it is a vision. It's real but "real" is our way of dismissing the strangeness. It's a way we keep mortality at bay. We're busy being busy. Sylvia knew that because she had been to the world of the dead and come back. What do you say to people? You write these odd little pieces that are tricked out in lines called "poems," but you are never quite back in the world of the living.

I know that's how I feel. When I came back to school from being institutionalized (the kind of word that Sylvia mocked), everyone tried to look at me and avoid me at the same time. They were cautious but friendly, curious but fearful. I knew they were pointing me out to those who didn't know what had happened: "Did you hear about Cathy?" I didn't blame them. I had crossed the line and my coming back didn't erase my having crossed the line. I'd like to say that everything is fine now and that I know I'll never go back to that dark, isolated place but I can't say that for sure. I can't say what put me there in the first place. There are dozens of pages of reports about me but those are observations and notions. They stem from the distance between any two people, particularly when the relationship is clinical. I'm still the body I am and that's still a mystery. That's why I need to have poetry in my life—it helps me with the mystery. It's a way of endlessly approaching it, a boat in pursuit of a floating island.

Well, it's not all mystery. Mrs. Pie Face is going over the bill with Ms. Forehand; they are deliberating over the tip. It's a funny thing to watch people deliberate over fifty cents. What is it about money that so unnerves us? Is it because it is finite and dear? Is it that we possess it but don't possess it anymore than we possess air or light? I don't know but these two women have the most serious expressions on their faces. You'd think they were pondering how many millions to give in foreign aid to some African country this year. They both pull back suddenly and smile: they've arrived at a decision. Have I been a good waitress? Has any extra dollar come my way? I can't wait to find out.

Sylvia had a tart tongue: "O I shouldn't put my finger in that / Auntie, it might bite!" She was full of practical joke mischief but full of mayhem, too. I wonder about the mayhem because I know it's in me. When I withdrew from the world, I turned it on myself. Destruction began at home. That's why I'm going to leave this beer-guzzling, burger-chowing town soon. I'm going to travel to far-off places and do some trekking—just me, my backpack and a pair of hiking boots. I want to do some dancing, also, so I'll bring a long dress and a pair of slippers. I want to keep my options open, though I don't plan on committing mayhem. It's more like I have to be in touch with how vast the mayhem is that has made this world. Geology is mayhem and geography is mayhem; it goes without saying that people are mayhem. On earth the mayhem can take billions of years but then it reaches that moment where the incredible happens—a tsunami or a volcano erupting or even a two-day, Great Plains blizzard. "Billions of years" are cardboard words. I need to feel that power more. I think that power can be a compass for me, one that can match the poetry compass.

Meanwhile, I'm looking at the mess that two women who probably weren't very hungry in the first place have left. There is coleslaw that left the plate, ketchup that flew, and lots of crumpled napkins. Among the debris are three one-dollar bills. Four dollars would have been extravagant. Generosity wouldn't want to step out of line and call attention to its lavish self. That other dollar will come in handy. That other dollar will save the Titanic and Judas and the passenger pigeon.

Is there more to life than the pathos of lipstick-smeared drinking glasses and crumpled dollar bills—our little gestures, reminders, and insistences?

The domesticity that goes with being female beguiled Sylvia, annoyed her, and oppressed her. She hated the pathos of the housewife. When I think of her by herself at the end with her children, I cringe. She was too honest to settle for writing poems as an end in its own right. She wanted to grab hold of the world and shake it till it fizzed. My MFA classmates want to be famous; they are full of ambition to win prizes and fellowships. They are going to have careers at universities. I feel like an anthropologist when they start blithely or worriedly chattering. Skating on perpetually thin ice is not the stuff of a career. I can imagine Sylvia daring herself, looking into the cutlery of despair—"Will you try this? And this?" It makes me too sad to think of it yet I admire her.

It's possible that my classmates' ice is thicker than mine is. Wiping tables dozens of times a day is good for me. It keeps me from residing in my head. I have to face the pathos of ordinariness, thoughtlessness, and indifference, of some ninny knocking the side of a glass with a knife. Someone has to clean up. I can mock myself and sometimes back at my apartment I look in the mirror and tease myself out loud. "What would you like to have for dinner, Cathy? The frozen tofu with Szechwan sauce is yummy. So is the dry cat food. Then there's the four-day-old salad in the back of the refrigerator you keep avoiding. A bit of mold gets a stomach going." I think I'm learning to write my way into that talk, the way that Sylvia learned to write her way into what was part goofy and part fierce. I'm on loan. I don't know for how long but then who does? I know that when you tell people how much you like Sylvia's poetry, they get nervous. "Didn't she kill herself? Does that mean you want to kill yourself? Does that mean you want to eat men like air? Does that mean you like fascists?" Sylvia was a high-wire act. She fell off a couple times and finally she fell off for good. Not many people want to walk on that wire high above the crowd. It's a rare soul who has the courage, the stamina, the intensity to want to be up there. It's an even rarer soul who can see herself doing it and joke about it. It's an impossible soul. That would have been Sylvia.

Audre Lorde, b.1934

I am the result of an experiment. My mother is of Irish-German descent (though I know that many, beginning with the British, have considered the Irish to be a poor excuse for white people); my father is African American. When I write the un-hyphenated "African American," I am giving you a political designation. According to the historical era and the social and linguistic awareness of the person speaking, my father could be called a person of color or a colored person or a Negro or a black or a capitalized Black, to say nothing of the vile, inventive panoply of racist slurs. His skin definitely isn't black. It's more like a toffee color. Imagine government forms on which you could write something under the heading of "skin tone" or you could choose from a menu of colors—toffee, umber, sepia, high yellow, Mississippi mud. Such crazy specificity would be a joke, which might not be a bad thing. I have suffered from enough overwrought seriousness about racial identity to last a few lifetimes. It's a tremor, however, that doesn't go away.

My parents married for love—or so they liked to tell me. I think they married out of a strange combination of sexual attraction and high-mindedness. I don't have to guess that fucking and social justice make for a weird combination. I know that it is a weird combination. One side of their identities was how they were all for getting down and having an open marriage. Both of them let it be known that they were heavy breathers, as my long-time friend Tamiko likes to call it. My father had more lovers than my mom, I'd guess, but she had her flings. Being sixties' types my parents made a point of being unashamed, uninhibited, and up front. I just wanted to get to my bedroom without some bozo asking me, "Whose little girl are you?" As an interracial child, I did not appreciate that question.

At the same time they were urgent people who believed that the world had to be made into a better place immediately, that every action every day made a difference. Some food or product was forever being boycotted in our house. I didn't taste a grape until I went to a classmate's house in the third grade. Some subtle political distinction was forever being decided. Though I didn't use the words on the playground, I understood at a too young age what "revisionist" and "tokenism" meant. Big actions made a difference, too. Revolution was in the air according to both of them (I was too little to brandish a placard myself) and they were not going to sit on the sidelines. They believed the time of justice was near. Maybe this was part of their religious heritages—both had Protestant moms who yearned for a heaven-sent apocalypse. I remember hearing about the movie called *Apocalypse Now* and thinking that must be about my parents. Revolution wasn't a promise; it was a fact. Now it seems as absurd as Audre Lorde, my mother's favorite poet-activist (the two words naturally went together for my mom), being invited to read at a presidential inauguration. Back then, though, everything seemed possible, even my parents' marriage.

They divorced when I was fourteen. They are both alive, but who they are now is different from who they were when I was growing up. They, as they both like to put it, "moved on," admitting however obliquely that the revolution didn't amount to more than a growl in the vast American night. They're pretty straight these days: my dad, who always loved languages, teaches Spanish in a high school and my mom is a yoga instructor. I, however, remain their daughter, a creature with dirty blonde, kinky hair, skin about midway between pale white and pale brown, and green eyes. I am sitting here in an airport lounge waiting for the delayed flight for Denver to take off and wondering, as often happens when I am at loose ends, whatever was going through their minds when they threw the caution that existed on both parental sides to the winds. Maybe it was love. That's the word we use when nothing else works. I'm not complaining; it's a better word than revolution.

I know my very different sets of grandparents loved me dearly. They didn't think much of their opposite number across the racial divide, but I was a reclamation project from the moment I drew breath. My father's parents thought my mom's parents were uppity white trash. My mom's parents thought my father's parents were hardworking but dim-witted sharecroppers who lived on peanuts and the intestines of pigs. When I was little, my parents made a show of gathering the family for Thanksgiving. They may have been Che-spouting revolutionaries, but both had a Norman Rockwell streak in them. Part of working for a better world meant going back to one that existed on a magazine cover in 1926. As a child I sensed the contradiction but was thankful for the food.

I think my grandparents were united in hating that day. Everyone tried reasonably hard, but cranberry relish wasn't going to move them beyond prejudices they had swallowed with their mother's milk. When they tried to make polite conversation, it was excruciating. Every word was taken as some evil, backhanded gambit. Meanwhile, my parents were shoving more turkey at everyone and making little jokes with one another to show how great everything was with them. Probably if my grandparents could have ducked out and gone to a bar, they might have been okay. They could have complained to one another about the foolish child they raised. But when I think back I doubt if there was any such bar around us where two such couples might have sat down and talked freely. "America is like an old movie," my father used to say, "black and white." He didn't sound bitter when he said that, just matter of fact. He, who married a white woman and walked down many a tense street with her hand in his, should know. I, who am indefinite, realized his pronouncements were one way he warded off the psychic assailants and that up to an unforgiving point they were true. Sometimes his love for me felt like pity.

During those abysmal holidays my grandparents took turns cooing over me. They had to know that I was in for a rocky road. Perhaps their adoration could make me strong. Neither pair was well off, but when it came to their granddaughter they were lavish. By the age of six I had dolls of every conceivable color. I could have played "Barbie Goes to the United Nations." My parents looked on tolerantly though they were careful to let me know that I was not a white person. How could I be when I looked at my father? When I looked in the mirror as a little girl I wondered who I was exactly. What doll factory had come up with my precise color? Who wanted to play with me? Where was my script and what were the right clothes? I've grown up but I'm still wondering. I'm sitting here watching Americans of all shapes and sizes and—yes—colors hurry by me to get to their destinations and part of me asks, "Who are you among these people?" Some days that questioning part of me feels like the whole of me.

That question was one the poet Audre Lorde asked again and again. Her parents were from the Caribbean. She was trying to make her way in white America the way every less than perfectly bland skin has to make his or her way in white America. It's not just earning a living, though when she was young Audre worked in a quartz crystal factory that may have given her the cancer that later in life killed her. It's your trying to retain who you are in a climate that has been obsessed with skin color while insisting that everyone is equal—or separate but equal. It's your being a square, racial peg looking for a color-blind, round hole. You can sand off some edges, but it's never going to be a clean fit. You can let your anger rip and make statements about what should be and believe that the revolution of right feeling is around the corner, but this country is too busy to listen. If it didn't listen when Martin Luther King, Jr., died, I don't think it's ever going to listen. One way I know that I must not be a white person is because I have a permanent grief inside me. They should have razed that block of Memphis and left it as eloquent, silent testimony. Or put up Audre's beautiful poem called "Rites of passage" that is dedicated to "MLK jr." and begins "Now rock the boat to a fare-thee-well." "Once we suffered dreaming," she wrote; now "we are growing through dream." I can't imagine this country putting up a poem like that in a public space. Some white man would start screaming that Audre was a lesbian colored woman. What America bestowed is official recognition—a new holiday. All he had to do was give up his life.

When they weren't displaying their love to one another by murmuring pet names or exchanging playful, tongue-revealing kisses, my parents were arguing. Geniuses of stubbornness, they asserted themselves about whatever was at hand—dill relish or sweet relish, Yankees or Dodgers, close the window or open the window, Richard Wright or James Baldwin. They threw themselves into every skirmish as if life depended on it. I guess life did. They were so busy validating one another as the crucial other half (what Audre appreciatively called "the difference") that they lost track of themselves. When a difference came along, they seized it with a righteous, thankful glee. I remember them throwing at one another the paperback books that were always near at hand. The symbolism of Eldridge Cleaver or Kate Millet flying through the air is too perfect for words.

Perhaps they argued so much because they agreed so intensely about some big things, such as racism being a virus in this country's soul. Their marriage was one way to kill that virus. Their most intimate feelings were enrolled in the overthrow of the bitter, racial paradigm. Their hearts were on the line; they were soldiers. Now that a degree of workaday sanity has entered their lives they have admitted that they took too much on. Having long ago sensed that my parents were Olympians in that department, I have nodded dutifully if sadly. Every day they devoured three or four newspapers. Every month they went through a dozen ugly-looking magazines with names that were redolent of political justice. I don't remember them sleeping much. "The revolution isn't going to happen with us sitting around on our asses," my father used to announce. They were on their asses quite a bit as they typed up letter after letter, but I understood the gist of what he was saying. Reading, writing, and thinking were a form of working.

I must have agreed because I became a philosophy student. That's a vocational ticket to nowhere so I had a double major—philosophy and accounting. I may have been the only such major in the history of my university. When I announced what I was doing to my mother and father, they both stared at me with something like hopeless disbelief. "Does philosophy mean political philosophy?" my dad asked with a trace of indignation in his voice. I told him I was more interested in moral philosophy. I was keen on Emerson and the Scottish Enlightenment. He shook his head. The very phrase "moral philosophy" seemed like another white shuck to him, a sideshow erected to avoid the real issues. As for accounting, it wasn't on either of their maps. When I was growing up, they eschewed checking accounts as "bourgeois." They used that word so much that Tamiko joked how my parents must be French. Meanwhile, they routinely lost cash they had put somewhere and then forgotten where that was.

I can't say numbers have saved me, but they've helped to anchor a life that has a lot of drift to it. I work for a corporate accounting firm. That's why I'm headed to Denver. I'll be looking at the columns and the ink, as they used to be called in the days before computers. Corporate people are super-polite with me. They've been through the workshops about racial propriety, to say nothing of harassment and discrimination. I know some of them go home and tell their wives and husbands about some smart, snoopy—you choose the racial noun—who came in today to work on an audit. But some of them don't; some of them don't think twice. That's the revolution I want: the revolution of human acceptance. Meanwhile, I smile a tight, all-business smile.

The airports I sit in make me think about Audre's airport poem. It was in her last book, the one that came out after she died. My mom sent me the book as a gift. That was sweet. She knew I thought a certain amount of Audre was revolutionary hooey because I had told her so. Attitudes age fast, especially ones that assume your political moment is for all time. Still, my mom loved Audre as someone who had battled with the complacent forces of evil. I agreed with her. I used to have a dartboard with Jesse Helms's face on it.

You wonder if the white world ever understands how much routine indignation is thrown our way and how we are supposed to grin and bear it. Audre had passion; in the zipped up world that I work in, I've come to appreciate that word. In my line of work you don't take chances because the "Man," as my father used to put it, is not paying you to take chances. It's the opposite. You nod at the right times, you pause at the right times and you speak about the matter at hand in a civil and direct way. No one wants uppity. Audre, who never took "no" for an answer from the white world, was uppity.

Audre's poem is short. It's called "Syracuse Airport":

Clean jeans and comfortable shoes
I need no secrets here   at home
in this echoless light
I spread my papers out
around me.

Opposite   alert

a grey-eyed lady takes fire
one pale nostril quivering
we both know women
who take up space
are called sloppy.

Since my parents argued about everything else, they argued about whether Audre was a poet. My dad said she wasn't. A poet according to him was someone like Paul Laurence Dunbar or Claude McKay, a man who wrote in the classic poetry style. He knew their best-known poems by heart and loved to recite them. "Now, this is poetry," he'd say and start in on "We wear the mask that grins and lies / It hides our cheeks and shades our eyes" or "When I have passed away and am forgotten / And no one living can recall my face." When my mom brought up a poet like Audre, my dad would get angry. "That isn't poetry! That's just some lines worming their way down a page. Poetry has a backbone. Poetry has an ancient sound. Poetry has dignity." He'd start sputtering, he would get so angry. I learned that you can be a cultural conservative and a political radical at the same time. Anyone who thinks a human being adds up to an even number is kidding herself.

My mom got angry right back at him. "Who the hell are you to tell the world what a poem is?" she'd ask him. "Where do you get off? And where do you get off telling a woman what to do?" When people ask me why my parents divorced, my one-word answer isn't "race"; it's "feminism." My dad came from the South; he thought women should be the chorus, not the soloists. To say my mom disagreed would have been a strenuous understatement. She upheld Audre as an example of what a poem by a woman could be. "Those lines worming their way down the page were written with a woman's heart and soul and blood—blood that leaves her body every month—and they have every right to exist. Do you hear me?" That last remark wasn't a question. She was yelling in his face.

Not that he backed down. "People do all kinds of things in this world, my lady. People write pages that are as disposable as paper towels and call them poetry. People ignore the fine traditions of African American writing so they can make up their own lax gobbledygook and call it poetry. People are afraid of strenuous feeling that is beautifully expressed. They'd rather spout." Even when I didn't agree with him I enjoyed my dad's vocabulary.

Sometimes my mom got a soft, happy look in her eyes when he called her "my lady." They could be very romantic. Other times, as when they were arguing, she got even madder. "Don't me call a lady! Don't evade what I'm telling you. That woman is a poet! And you are as smug as the day is long!" My parents acted as though assertions were bulldozers that could raze any wrongheaded thought in their way. When Tamiko used to sleep over, she'd say, "I hope your parents get in an argument. It's exciting." Her parents were Japanese. Tamiko said they threw "quiet daggers" at one another.

It's little wonder that I wear conservative suits, enjoy parsing a financial statement, and read Emerson's "Nominalist and Realist" for pleasure. Emersonian possibility sits well with me. I crave room to breathe and imagine who I am. I like his well-mannered excitement. He is one of those white men who sense there is more to life than being a white man. The gift of Audre, though, has stayed with me. When I look at a poem like "Syracuse Airport," I understand my dad's feelings. It's casual and seems almost broken down. I guess that's because Americans of all colors are casual and broken down. One look at the people lurching around this airport in their sweatshirts and polyester confirms that. But that's not the whole of it. If you refuse to wear the mask, if you put yourself out there, then the way you inscribe that vulnerability isn't going to necessarily sound like Paul Laurence Dunbar or Claude McKay. Especially, if you acknowledge yourself as a woman—someone who is always supposed to be tidying up and smoothing out life's ugly wrinkles—then you are not going to sound like a mellifluous gentleman. A moment—someone spreading her papers out in an airport—is no big thing and doesn't want to be written out as a big thing, but the moments are what we have. Big things—witness Emerson's transparent eyeball—have their place but the small things have to be given their due. If those are "women's things"—as my father would put it with barely concealed contempt in his voice—then so be it.

Yet what goes down in that poem is a big thing. It's about being a woman, being Black (Audre's spelling—I prefer the lower case "b") in public. It's about attending to yourself when you need to attend to yourself, in the way you need to attend to yourself. It's about identity because your skin color is always there in other people's eyes. It's like your first skin should be your second skin, too—a protection from itself. Or it's like your shell is your insides. Or it's like letting down that famous mask and being merely an everyday person. Trying to put this into sentences makes me feel why there is poetry. Whether it's Langston Hughes or Audre Lorde, it's the words beyond the words.

I'm on the lookout in these airports for that "grey-eyed lady" who "takes fire." A lot of people live to be intolerant. It's a pleasure to them, a sick one but a pleasure. Life dumps on you, but you can rise above your shame by rising above someone else—particularly if that someone else is an African American, female stranger. I'm dressed in a suit that says that it costs money so I am safe on that count. The suit says that I am someone who may be important, which causes another kind of trouble. I can sense the indignation out of the corner of my eye: who is this nigger woman fooling? Doesn't she know she's a nigger? But she doesn't exactly look like a nigger with that hair and that skin. Maybe she's isn't a nigger. What is she then? I can see these thoughts picking at a white woman's mind as she tries to focus on her magazine or roots through her pocketbook for something that wasn't there in the first place. I can feel her being responsible for the upkeep of the white race and the degradation of the black one. It's a full time job. Sometimes the woman sighs. I feel like giving her a candy bar and telling her that it's okay, she doesn't have to work so hard.

Being African American means you have paranoia in your genes. It's intelligent paranoia, though, because it's made of self-protection, caution, and wariness. Every African American is a public figure because every African American exists as an idea in white people's minds. It's no wonder that I took up philosophy. To be African American is to be a mental construct with a physical body. That's a neat but unhappy trick. Audre understood that; she became what she already was anyway—a public figure. My dad said she was always on a soapbox but who was he to talk?

My hero Emerson felt that each of us has the right and obligation to be who we are and not scrimp about it. As he wrote about nature: "She will have all." Audre was nature; she never scrimped. When she spread her papers out in the airport, she was showing the world that she had the right to take up her space. As much as many white folks didn't want for someone like her to exist, she wasn't going to be bustled off any stage. She knew that you have to inhale and exhale the same air as the white folks. She knew that you have a right to that air. "If John was perfect, why are you and I alive?" wrote Emerson. John was a white man, believe me.

Though the people in this airport are mostly dressed dreadfully, Americans are awash in money. At this juncture they are the winners of capitalism. In a generation they may be the losers, but right now they are on a tear. They don't know what to do with it especially, but then they aren't reading Emerson to think about how they should conduct their lives. They don't look very pretty but money doesn't make you pretty. You have to make yourself pretty. If I dressed like some of these women in their pastel pantsuits, I'd live in a rabbit hole. They've given up or gone back to childhood.

My mother says I'm too hard on everyone, beginning with myself. Unlike me, she wasn't born with the imp of definition on her back. Unlike me she doesn't find herself standing in an airport bathroom and staring at herself. Who is this woman in the mirror: a black white woman or a white black woman or someone who can't be explicated, someone who has fallen through a large historical crack, someone who can pass for a ghost? However much the face looks back at me, I don't quite believe that I exist.

You don't have any say about your being brought into this world. The spirituals used to proclaim that—black folks didn't ask to be brought into the woe that awaited them. You do have to find yourself, though, in this world. You have to locate your soul, which is tricky if you have a face like mine. A face is what you take for granted. You stop looking at yourself except to scrutinize the surfaces—eyebrows too thick or lips chapped. You know that face; it's your double and it's your single. But I don't stop looking at myself. Someone in this bathroom might think I'm a first-class narcissist. "Get away from that mirror, girl! You look good enough!" If only I were the sum of my vanity.

Beauty isn't the issue. More than one man has assured me of that without any qualifications or footnotes. And I know that a mirror is a bad place to search for your soul. But I know, too, that I am always being looked at and that the mirror is my truest metaphor. I get to look and I get to look back at myself. I get to be a world unto myself except that I don't know what—beyond my being a living hypothesis—that world is. My mom tells me I worry too much, but she gave over a portion of her life to showing that this racial sleight-of-hand could be figured out as if it were an emotional algebra equation. Love and tenacity would solve all. That's not what the mirror says. The mirror says that the looking does not stop nor does the judging. You are a fool if you think otherwise.

That's why the story of Emmett Till is so important. Audre wrote about it in her poem "Afterimages," where she got the feeling right though she got some details wrong. The story is the basic one: a black boy "insults" a white woman. He whistled at a young woman as he was leaving a store. He was a fun-loving boy, full of jazz. Maybe he was showing off. Maybe he was letting himself go. Maybe he was just being a young man. The white woman got angry and told her husband. Her husband and another man pulled fourteen-year-old Emmett out of bed and beat him brutally, shot him, and threw him in a river. The murderers got off scot-free. Emmett's mother, whose husband had died in World War II in the cause of American freedom, lost her only child on a "vacation" to Mississippi. She left the coffin open in the Chicago church so people could see what the ways of white folks had done: here is how a boy's whistle has been avenged. I wonder how many people in white America said that Emmett Till got what was coming to him. How many people said, "Look at what the Nazis did and the communists—seas of blood. What is one black boy?"

My mother told me that story when I was a girl. It's not a bedtime story, but the fact of my parents' marriage dispelled bedtime stories with inevitably happy endings. I was raised to know how bad the worst could be because the worst—the deep well of prejudice—was part of their lives and, by implication, part of mine. That didn't seem fair to me. What had I done that I had to take Emmett Till's death to heart? I didn't live in Mississippi and had no intention of visiting. That had all happened in the past—before black people took their destiny into their own righteous hands. It still doesn't seem fair to me but part of me (everything with me comes in parts) is good with it. Innocence is a terrible thing to carry through life because it's bound to be willful. Your innocence is based on someone else's degradation. Your innocence means you are canceling out the fact of evil. Any moral philosopher would tell you that innocence is thoughtlessness. That's why it's so appealing; that's why it's so hurtful. Everyone wants to look away now and then, but you can't make a life from looking away.

Nor can you make your life be about looking at evil. Thinking too long about the terrible things that people do to other people can make you crazy. My parents thought their striving goodness would cancel out the evil around them, that bitter eye that fixed them as they walked down the street holding hands. When you hear the expression "evil eye," you understand how much resides in looking, how the eye casts spells. Young Emmett Till went beyond the looking. He whistled. Imagine—he made a sound! He wasn't mute but muteness has been more than enough. Black men were lynched for looking at a white woman too directly. They didn't touch the woman. They didn't speak a word. They looked at her—but looking is all it takes.

Looking is at the center of the uncertainty I inherited. I'm not going to be murdered for looking, but I recognize that looks can kill. I've been around enough public places to know. That's where Audre shines. In her poem about Emmett Till she writes, "my eyes are always hungry." That's one part of the looking. You can't get enough of life. Our human eyes are greedy, but there's another truth in that phrase, which is that black people are bound to have hungry eyes because they can't partake of white America the way that whites can. They can have their share in certain ways but only in certain ways. Go tell your eyes that they are separate but equal. Like Audre's, my eyes are hungry. Looking in the mirror at myself, I feel that hunger—as if my eyes could see further. My father told me Superman should have been black because black people know the most about X-ray vision.

In the poem Audre averts her eyes from the "pornography" of the descriptions and photos in magazines of Emmett Till's ruined body. Later she writes that she is "betrayed by vision." If she wrote nothing more than that phrase, Audre would matter to me because that phrase is the truth. Though it occurs in a poem, that phrase is moral philosophy. That phrase is the ember that gets carried around every day in my heart. "Seeing is believing," we say, but we believe what we want to believe. If you are honest—and at her best Audre was as honest as anyone who ever picked up a pen—you have to admit that our vision is flawed by our wanting. We inherit the "afterimages" Audre names her poem for, the flickering visions that compose memory and fantasy and longing and regret and anger. There they are—burned into us. There is Emmett Till's body and the unbearable, everyday situation of people looking at what they cannot see and acting on their savage, mythical non-sense. There is Audre Lorde, "betrayed by vision" but alive to words.

My parents assumed that someone who knew about Emmett Till would grow up and work for justice. What else could such a person work for—a soulless corporation? I remember yelling at them one night during one of the post-divorce, family dinners they both insisted on to show me they were still friends. "I am justice," I shouted, "and I have to live with it!" I remember their regarding me with wide eyes. It had never occurred to them.

The flight to Denver is in no hurry. Here in Boston it's a clear, not-a-cloud-in-the-sky day but in Denver it's snowing. I need a magazine to divert my thoughts from my thoughts. I need to let my eyes feast on glossies of clothes and shoes and hair. I need to let myself dally in the realms of smiling perfection. I like clothes and I'm not embarrassed about it. People are looking. I'm glad to give them something to see.

I don't get up, though, because I can feel some eyes. It's a white lady in her late sixties—a common culprit. She's sitting opposite me but there's a good-sized aisle between us. She's not clever about it. I can see her peering above the *USA Today* she is supposedly reading. They are hazel eyes, not soft but not beady either. They are average informers, common spies. What she's reading is me. I meet those eyes casually as if to say, "I see you, too," but she doesn't flinch. Though she's looking hard at me, I don't seem to be there. In the annals of my provocative nonexistence that's not unusual but remains unsettling. She's seeing through me or she's thinking some racial thought that has blocked me out or she has resolved to not let me turn her gaze away. I might as well be a sculpture or a vista or a specimen. Yet she needs me. I turn to a farther scene, a board with flight information, but she continues as if she were a sentinel, as if her curiosity had every right.

I find myself exhaling but when I look back at her with unfeigned directness, as in Two Can Do This, she's disappeared behind newsprint. I see only a headline—"Country Headliners Come Home to Nashville." I see some white faces in the paper below the headline. They are smiling. They know a camera is looking at them; as stars all they have to do is smile their pleasant, self-satisfied smiles. I'm not a hater but I understand how some black people wind up as haters. A camera is looking at me, too, but it never gets turned off. No one cares if I smile or not.

Someday I will get used to this—the drama of nothing happening and something obscurely enormous happening. Someday all the envisioning that goes with being in a public place will leave me cold and unaffected. Someday I will know so well who I am that gazes will fall off me like leaves from an autumn tree. I will be bare and free. That's what I tell myself and I half-believe it. This nation is an experiment; I certainly am part of it. Most days the nation is content to look and not touch. Most days it fumbles along unless some scrap of fear and loathing, of "the difference" comes out. It could be a woman setting out her papers on a seat in an airport. It could be a boy whistling. It could be a pair of green eyes. It's that crazy. It's that poetic.

Joe Bolton, b.1961

W.H Auden is supposed to have replied to casual inquiries about his vocation with the numbing remark, "I am a professor of medieval history." One imagines Auden's interlocutor, someone traveling on a train and looking for a bit of light, engaging conversation, straining a responsive smile and muttering something agreeable ("must be fascinating") before diving back into the habitual safety of a newspaper or novel. To say that Auden disliked the popular afflatus that went with the word "poet" would be an understatement. Who can blame him? The word has more dubious connotations than Dalmatians have spots. To a wary soul such as Auden the notion of having to explain a calling at once recondite—"I don't really get poetry; maybe you can explain it to me"—and readily available—"I've written a poem or two, Mr. What-Did-You-Say-Your-Name-Was"—must have been very unappetizing. Better to evoke the castle gate of a long-ago era and let it fall between you and any curious fellow passengers. Better to seem incorrigibly dusty.

I've been flying to Phoenix frequently over the past year and a half because my father has been sick with emphysema. I hate Phoenix. Everyone goes into raptures about the desert, but it's too hot and there aren't any trees and there shouldn't be so much concrete and so many people in the middle of what is clearly intended to be nowhere. I feel a sunny ugliness in Phoenix, the sense of people who have moved here from elsewhere and are choking on their self-congratulation. The cold, gray misery they felt in Buffalo or Chicago can be laid to rest here. I can feel the lizards' indignation.

Even with his compromised lungs, my dad is an incorrigible go-to guy. He had to give up smoking, but he's busy praising the air conditioning in his apartment. The vanquishing of the heat thrills him. "Is this cool, delicious air, Baron, or is this cool, delicious air?" I agree with him. He's a connoisseur who rates restaurants and movie theaters not on their food or films but on their air conditioning. Sometimes I feel that he wasn't an accountant in his life up north but a refrigerator repairman. The desert has given him a whole other perspective. If, as the Buddhists believe, focusing on your breath is a path to enlightenment then my dad is bucking for bodhisattva. His cough makes me feel that death is moments away.

When I look around his little apartment whose decor consists largely of oxygen canisters and aquariums (my dad has always liked tropical fish), I see some books of poetry I once gave him. The better part of a sixteenth of an inch of dust has come to rest on them. My dad isn't much for cleaning what wants to be left undisturbed. Still, he hasn't thrown them into a garbage pail or an incinerator. "It's not going to compete with TV or Hollywood," he once told me when I informed him that my first book of verse was going to be published. I could hear the treble of parental determination in his voice. He was letting me down easy. He was telling me one of those home truths a parent has to impart. His voice had a wise, reasonable gentleness that I loved. I agreed with him and shook my head with grateful resignation. Anything a son and father can agree upon is precious.

The poet Joe Bolton died in Arizona. He killed himself—a gun in his mouth. He was twenty-eight. He knew he wanted to kill himself but that wasn't a big thing to know. He could have let himself live longer and try to learn something else but he had a thick, blue cloud over his head. He must have seen the sun like everyone else, but I'm not sure. When you say the word "poet," you are implying someone who doesn't see the sun like everyone else. William Blake is a famous case in point. He saw angels and emanations in the sun. Poets carry their own weather. They're not very good at being obliging. They have other errands.

I haven't given my father Joe Bolton's book of poetry because of the dust that already has accrued to the wry, beautiful titles that sit beside the ceramic donkey his second wife made in an adult education pottery class. The titles shimmer like heat mirages. You don't see the word "heaven" much outside of church, but poetry is still using it: *Refusing Heaven, No Heaven, Raw Heave*n. Poetry hangs in there. It believes in disbelief. When I was younger, I thought curiosity might get the better of Dad and he would pick one up. Accountants, however, treasure routines and reports. Any enterprise that can't be summarized isn't worth bothering with. Like totems of a forgotten religion the slim volumes scintillate. When I look at them, I feel the pangs of my erstwhile naiveté and longing. Years ago I switched for Father's Day to high-tech thrillers whose authors seem to be paid by the pound.

I have read poems aloud to him. At the end of a long, wheezing day, when he lies back on his living room couch, he will listen to anything—even poetry. He looks then like a vigorous rag doll—ruddy complexion but his stuffing is coming out. When I tell him I'd like to read him a poem, he raises an index finger and twirls it around—an ironic bit of whoopie. Life has brought him to this impasse—a wrung-out old man whose son subjects him to poetry.

Because it has a father and son theme, I read Joe's poem "Watching Bergman Films with My Father":

What you can't quite appreciate
In angles, lighting, and camera work,
You make up for
With your deep understanding of despair,
The gray that flickers in the dark
And fingers your gray face.

It's nothing new to you, really,
This sense of loss at things falling away,
Life in shadow.
You've felt everything that you're feeling now
And lived these scenes in your own way,
Only less artfully.

And so you're not surprised that the girl
Goes mad in God's absence, or that the man
Just shoots himself
By the river, or that the smoke and filth
Choking the lungs of a woman
Almost isn't painful

Seen from this distance. We don't talk

About it or talk about anything.
Outside, the sky
Is preparing to darken and to die
Without color, stars. Everything
Is ready for the walk

We'll take because there's nothing else
To do, because we need the world, if it
Doesn't need us.
Despite our differences, there isn't much
Difference between us tonight,
And there's nobody else.

I like there to be some silence after a poem is read, some time to take it in and be with it. That's not my dad's style, though. "So," he starts in, "what's with poetry? I know it's meant a lot to you, but it's not very strong in the answers-to-life's-problems-department, is it? What's the good of that?" My father's eyes are lasered on mine. "What's the good of that?" He enjoys the rhetorical flourish of a repetition. He smiles—not vindictively but not happily either. Something real is eating at him.

"Literature is the question, Dad. There are no answers."

"Phooey!" he sputters. "No answers? Come on. There must be answers. Why should I read questions? I have too many of them and I'm an *alter kocker*. I should know better. I'd like to know what's on the other side—there's a question for you."

I make a point of being patient. "Maybe, there are questions you haven't thought of. Maybe those questions would dispel other questions." Though I know I shouldn't, I tend to get hopeful with my dad. It's a yearning that must be imprinted in the souls of sons. He's been all business forever. When we're together, I want something more than business.

"Maybe, maybe, maybe. I'm tired of maybe. Maybe doesn't take you very far down life's road. Look at this Joe Bolton. According to you he killed himself at the ripe old age of twenty-eight. Twenty-eight! I was still wet behind the ears at twenty-eight."

"Does he sound wet behind the ears to you, Dad?" The vise that holds the two of us is starting to tighten. I can feel it.

From my father I get a long, pointed look of parental regard. It's somewhere between Job and a situation comedy. That's a big space, but I can't define it further because it touches on both sides of that divide. "No, he doesn't sound wet behind the ears at all. He sounds as though life has been a waiting room with him sitting there too long with nothing to do. He sounds gray." Suddenly, my dad makes a sort of keening sound. I'm not sure if it's derision or his collapsing lungs. Probably it's both. "He should have had a job besides writing poetry. A job would have straightened him out."

"What if he didn't want to be straightened out? What if poetry was his job?"

From his protracted pause I can tell that my father is treating my questions as if studying an alien form of life. To a degree it amuses him that I am so different. Our cataclysmic arguments are behind us. I have gone my way and he has held to his course, but we both know the terrain. Our differences now are more rueful than dramatic.

"Did you like the poem, Dad? Anything move you?"

"I liked that he was with his father just the way I like it when you show up here even though I know you can't stand this place. I like that." He regards me and smiles. His eyes emit a faraway look—something he can see that I can't see. He starts rocking slightly. A coughing fit is about to commence.

"I'm glad, Dad." And that is that—another draw, not exactly amiable but not unamiable. Our shared manhood lurches on into the night.

Every poetry workshop I have ever taught has had more women in it than men. It's something that almost goes without saying: women have feelings and need to write poems and men have—what? Men have their stubbornness, their aggressions, their competitions, their implacable certainties. Men have the world to remodel as they see fit. Poetry, however, remodels nothing. Poetry is the admission of the vulnerable tremor that runs through each moment. Most men don't want that admission. In refusing poetry, they say, as my dad says, they don't need that admission. They don't need to enter those domains; they don't need to admit their feelings. Their feelings will take care of themselves, which tends to mean either burial or explosion. Yet men, including young men such as Joe Bolton, have written countless moving and powerful poems.

Maybe that's because for men (I don't presume to speak for women) poetry comes from an impossible place. It's the place where, as a man, you aren't supposed to go but you need to go. To dwell on feelings is a weakness because feelings exist to be overcome. Yet as you indulge the perquisites of language, that dwelling is a strength. It's a very mixed message that you, as a man, are being given and are giving off. And language is an equivocal force; words aren't sticks and stones. Little wonder that many poets have glowed with inner conflict. I think of Homer's Achilles as a poet—sulking in his tent, moody, prideful, and refusing to be a warrior. Then he learns of Patroclus' death and he acts. Wrath is a sure feeling. It is his moment to deal death. Death, as in the lamentations heard on the plain of Troy, furthers feeling.

Joe Bolton was on a death trip. Though he moved around America, attending various writing programs—havens that licensed his muse—his poems go nowhere. He is stuck in the miasma of transience. It's a beautiful miasma, however. We wouldn't appreciate anything without it. Transience gilds every moment. Underneath those moments, as Bolton loved to intuit, death is sticking out its impudent tongue and murmuring sweet, dissolute nothings. Poetry, as my dad likes to point out, is no help in this department. The condition of our transience is best forgotten or ignored or annealed by religion. How could we live otherwise? How could we bear the weight of nothingness? For someone such as Joe Bolton transience wormed its way into his anguished, self-aware bones. He felt the drift of his biology, what used to be called "the human condition."

Poetry is tied to our pulses; it's rooted in biology. Yet language is elsewhere. The conflict between the two, their never quite coming together, makes poetry. The pulse insists on life's primacy. We take it for granted. Our pulse is not an explanation; it's a condition, yet language insists on our explaining ourselves: words are justifications. Language is a condition, too, but because we are defined by it ("in the beginning was the Word"), it is one that we can never leave. Why would we? It empowers and teases us. Joe Bolton adored the words, loved even "despair" as a word—the hardness of the "d" modified by the wary softness of the "sp," the calmness of the word, the loss of hope at the root of the word, the stern, sad dispensations of etymology. To live with the words the way poets live with the words is to invite the illuminating uncertainties of time at each fraught step. Something vast is in every packet of sound.

That's not much help in day-to-day life. Poets haven't been notably good at day-to-day life. Joe Bolton, who pursued the usual bad habits with self-destructive zeal, was not good at it. Being haunted by time doesn't help you do the laundry or buy groceries. Being haunted tends toward obsession; obsession tends to shut down the simple, middling doors that open onto other people's lives. Poets carry a sack on their backs stuffed with language and feeling, a sack that is bound to get in the way. It's a comic vision except that it's near tragic—how the sack is precious yet onerous.

Whether any of this is reason enough to kill yourself is something that my dad who is hanging onto life with some serious, odds-defying tenacity would laugh out loud at. I can hear him crowing, "Give me a break," in his genial schmuck manner. I can't blame him. Doing away with yourself for metaphysical reasons seems both perverse and arcane. And yet there are creations like Bergman's films that are about obsession and haunting, about how people become unnerved, about the underground river that flows beneath the mild dailiness of life. Plenty of people live their whole lives and never sense that river. Or they act as though they never sense it; they pretend. Meanwhile, there are the poets sending their kinesthetic dispatches: "Feel this" or "Look at that" or the praise of "Wow!" or the agony of "Never!"

When you encounter those dispatches for the first time, when you read Dylan Thomas or Lorca or Gerard Manley Hopkins or Sylvia Plath, it can move the ground beneath your feet. When I read Lorca in high school, I thought, "This is it. This is who I am. This thrills me. Whatever this poetry place is, I want to live there." Maybe someone has studied why this happens; why one person reads Lorca and gets excited and another reads Lorca and goes, "What the hell?" More likely that other person—a person such as my father—never makes it to Lorca. It's terra incognita. It doesn't even shimmer on the horizon.

What you intuit when you are young and reading the poets for the first time is that the stories about the poets—the squalor and the quiet glory and the price that one way or another gets paid—are true. They seem like legends—Coleridge on laudanum and Walt Whitman walking the streets of Manhattan and Emily Dickinson in her room and Yeats attending seances and Hart Crane aboard that final boat—but they are true. Poets don't have to live those legends, but if you don't enter into some degree of the legendary, of something larger and deeper than anecdotes, then I don't see how a poet is a poet. The poet is the person who takes on the feelings that the society is ignoring or suppressing or bartering or jettisoning and who makes them whole. Those feelings comprise legends—the Abandoned Daughter or the Camerado of the Open Road—that inform the poet's life. Even when the poet is shattered, the feelings strive toward wholeness. Even when the poem itself seems shattered, as in *The Waste Land*, a wholeness is at work. And wholeness is the most legendary of human enterprises. It posits that we can exist like a bird or a tree—perfect in our being yet as humans aware of our flaws and contradictions. It posits that there is a coherence that we can tap into that is vaster than we are—yet of which we, as abiders on earth, partake. Even our longings are part of it. If poetry gives up on wholeness, it turns against itself.

In terms of the legends, Joe Bolton might be designated the Emperor of Longing. My dad wouldn't get that; there's no reason he should. You spend your adult life doing a job and making the money that enables you to merge your needs with your desires. This work keeps you sensibly busy. Joe Bolton, however, never emerged from the cocoon of longing, never obliged a routine. You can say that he was immature but that doesn't seem fair. He clearly worked hard at the poems. He got poetry in the most essential way, how it picks up the biggest conscious burden—time passing—and goes off whistling, full of the pleasure of language. What he didn't get was the rest of the world, which could not have cared less about poetry. What he didn't get was why other people weren't moved the way he was moved. What he didn't get was how most people were trying to make the days into a chain of plausible reasons. He was making his days into a chain of losses—glowing, inveigling, and pearly remorse. Though I assume he wanted love, I don't think he understood it in the sense of accepting another human being as something other than a fantasy. He wanted to pine forever, yet he knew "forever" was a lie.

On the plane out to Phoenix I read a Bolton poem called "Elegy at Summer's End":

Now the darker cloth is drawn from closets,
The summer dresses put away
Whose flowers fade faster than even summer's own.
Now a minor music begins:
First frost and newfound clarity of sky.

I've left you sleeping in the summerhouse
To walk the loved edge of the lake
Where the southward flight of geese is more heard than seen,
As this summer may come to seem
A season less remembered than invented.

Already there have been too many words,
Too many versions of the way
The light fell across the water some certain dusk
And the "stunned" trees on the far shore
Caught fire: *candescence, conflagration, blaze.*

Now the darker cloth is drawn from closets,
And we who loved the world must learn

The language of absence: days foreshortened, empty rooms,
The irrevocable distance
Between the goodbye and the letting go.

The woman next to me was reading *Newsweek* intently. She was in her late fifties, had an intelligent face, and worry lines etched between her eyebrows—a habitual furrower. The secretary of state, whose picture was on the cover, had just resigned. He looked pretty tired, as if he had been up a lot of nights but not partying. He looked as though he had done too much thinking and talking. I wondered how many secretaries of state I had seen come and go in my lifetime. They participate in some big decisions; then most of them vanish into the gloaming. It can't be easy looking after the rest of the world, particularly in a country like the United States, which barely knows there is a rest of the world. I've met more than one person who didn't know there were other countries on the continent, who thought the United States was it for North America. That wasn't this *Newsweek* reader, however, who put the magazine down slowly and let out a discernible sigh. The world was not in good shape. She had taken on a few more ounces of that oppressive yet carefully explicated confusion.

"Nations are thugs," I offered by way of introduction.

She looked quickly at me. I don't have a particularly forbidding face but who knew what was behind my remark? I could have been anything. Lately, I have been thinking about the intriguing coinage "narco-terrorist." Maybe I was one of those. She sniffed and acted as though she hadn't heard me.

"Someone has to bat someone else around, I guess. Someone has to give it up, too." I thought I sounded like a street-wise pundit, though that seems a contradiction in terms. I don't follow world politics, but I understand the gist of what is usually going down—the frequently fatal opera of distrust and threats, bombast and lies. It's strained manners, tight smiles, bluff handshakes, anger heaving in hotel rooms late at night, contempt. Standard knowledge says that poets are out of it and in some ways they are, as with Joe

Bolton writing one poem after another with some variation of the word "dark" in it. He couldn't leave the word alone and the word wouldn't leave him alone. Yet for all their myopia, most poets aren't inclined to go fishing in the worthless ponds of international imbroglio. And why compound it by reading about disingenuous people whom you'll never meet anyhow when you can meet words in poems? Poets are looking for the news about being alive. There's no telling where you will find this news nor is there any requisite protocol, which is part of poetry's no-press-conferences charm. As I noted, it's legendary.

"You sound like a cynic. Are you a cynic? Cynics are people who enjoy being disagreeable. Do you enjoy being disagreeable?" She drew herself up in her seat as if she were pleased with the tartness she had just let loose. I got the feeling she played tennis seriously. I could imagine her preparing to serve, going into that state of concentration where the body is a bow and the ball is an arrow.

"Do you play tennis?" I asked her.

Her jaw didn't drop, but it wasn't the comeback she expected.

"As a matter of fact, I do. Do you play?"

"No, but I've been interested in tennis forever. I don't know why I've never taken it up. I can't stand golf and it seems if you can't stand golf, you should play tennis. Sort of like putting your money where your mouth is."

We bobbed for some seconds in a conversational trough, neither of us speaking. A fair amount of random provocation had already been put out on the table.

"I'm not a cynic. Granted that self-definitions are largely worthless, but still I'm not what anyone would call a cynic. To tell the truth, I tend to idealism."

She may have wanted to talk about tennis further. I could feel some tennis longing in a twitch at the corners of her mouth. Being a poet and one who is fond of Joe Bolton, I have fairly good radar in regards to longing. I could see her bouncing on her toes, alert and ready to receive service. She was a serious soul, though, and let it go. "Don't you want the world to be a better place," she asked. "Don't you care? Don't you think we need to get along with one another?" She had a lot of questions for someone who looked so composed. Her dress didn't have a wrinkle; it looked like real cotton.

"Actually, I think the world is a pretty good place already. I don't see how it could get much better. I mean there are birds and we have eyes that see and spring comes every year. It's pretty swell." I grinned a goofy, contented grin.

She gave me a long, narco-terrorist stare. "I don't believe you."

"That's your prerogative but look at what I'm reading." I pointed to the volume of Joe Bolton's poems. "It's poetry."

She looked at the book then she looked down at her *Newsweek* with its photo of the departing secretary of state on the cover. The secretary of state looked more tired and baleful than ever, as if being on this plane ride had worn him out further.

"Are you a poet?"

It's reasonable to ask someone with a book of poetry that question because who else reads poetry? I wasn't going to tell her I was a historian of the Middle Ages. She might know something about the Middle Ages. Then I'd be in trouble because I don't know when exactly Thomas Aquinas lived or what constituted a fiefdom. "Yeah, I'm a poet."

"What's that like?" She turned slightly in her seat so as to fix her full attention on me. She had deep brown eyes. There was some gray in her hair. I like it when women let it be and don't dunk their heads in some brittle, simulated color. She smiled very slightly. I'm a fool for a thoughtful woman's smile.

"It's a longer story than this plane ride but briefly—it's okay. No one particularly knows who you are or what you are doing. You spend a lot of time thinking about words. You think a poem is done and then you wake up another day and realize it's not done at all, so it keeps you on your toes. That's good, don't you think, to keep on your toes?"

She nodded. It was a safe question, because I knew she liked to be on her toes. I could see her in her tennis shoes and those little anklet socks.

"You spend a lot of time reading other poets. It's sort of like a club, though it's hard to imagine many of them getting along with one another because they tend to be high-strung. Poets get vibrations." I wondered what I was talking about and felt like some New Age airhead trying to describe the indescribable. Involuntarily I clicked my tongue against the roof of my mouth. Maybe I should have boned up on Chartres and the Magna Carta.

"Are you high-strung?"

"No, actually, I'm not. Again, you can't trust self-definition, but for a poet I'm easy-going." I paused. "I chew on the bone of grief a fair amount but nothing inordinate. And I'm pleased with the world—the birds and springtime, what I said before to you when you said you didn't believe me."

"Was the poet you are reading pleased with the world?"

By way of an answer, I read "Elegy at Summer's End" to her. Afterwards, I told her that I'd never read a poem to someone on an airplane before.

"It's beautiful," she said. There was feeling in her voice, a soft, taut register that hadn't been there before. "Is the whole book like that?"

"Pretty much. Life was an elegy for this guy. He could see time passing and he felt it. Not many people like it when summer is over because the darkness is coming but they don't write a poem about it. They go ahead and live with it. This guy wrote poems about those things. Lots of them."

"Is this poet—what's his name?"

"Joe Bolton."

"Is he alive?"

"No, he died some years ago." There was that awkward pause that the mention of death causes. She may have wanted me to say more but I didn't feel like it. Mortality casts enough of a cloud already.

"I'm going to sit here and look out the window at the sunlight but I want to thank you for reading that to me. No one has read me a poem since I was a little girl. That's a while ago." She smiled again. "Thank you." She had very even teeth. Usually that scares me, the presence of smiling perfection, the mix of money and genes, but her teeth didn't scare me.

She nodded politely but more than that, too, more like a confirmation, more like recognizing something inside of herself. Then she turned the other way and snugged her left shoulder into the seatback. I figured she wanted to be quiet and go into a dream. I could understand that. It was one reason to read poetry in the first place, to enter that place between "the goodbye and the letting go." I went back to Joe Bolton's darkness.

That evening, I told my dad what had happened. He asked me if I told the woman who I was or tried to find out who she was. I said that I hadn't.

He leaned back on the living room couch and looked perplexed. "You're not much of one for connecting with strangers, are you? You're not what they call a 'networker' these days. Even when you're not in your study, you're in your study." He made a low, harumphing sound. On the chart of my dad's sounds that one means "When is this kid going to get a clue?" That I'm not a kid makes it worse.

"It was a conversation, Dad. I don't have many about poetry with people in airplanes. Usually they're reading a newspaper or snoring. I thought you'd get a kick out of it. You know, someone being interested in poetry."

"Maybe she was being polite. People act polite when they don't know what else to do." He paused. "Some funny things come out of your mouth."

"What are you talking about?" Like that, I was on my feet and more or less yelling. My dad is still waiting for me to wake up. The poetry spell will be over. Then I will be a real, entrepreneurial, get-ahead, pockets-full-of-money American. I will be done with my imagining. I will be in that blessed, vegetal yet earnest state called "normal."

"It's a sensible thing to say, Baron. It's what you say to a child who is no longer a child but who often acts like one."

It's not as though we haven't been down this shoddy road. I've rehearsed it with more than one therapist. In his poem about watching the Bergman film Joe Bolton could share the despair. I keep mine in a metaphorical drawer. I ask him if he's afraid I'll throw myself out a window or put a gun in my mouth.

He's quiet. Death is on his own doorstep; he doesn't take the subject lightly. "I worry. I've always worried. You worry the most about what you understand the least." He stops. He raises his hands as if feeling toward an object. "Sometimes from what you tell me, I think that you feel death is the price you have to pay for being a poet. Would that be a fair thing to say?"

"Death is part of the equation. Maybe it's more part of the equation than for most people. Death makes poetry possible because poetry loves transience. Poetry loves that we can't hold on to what we want to hold onto. Poetry isn't fatalistic or indifferent. Poetry loves what goes by. Is there something wrong with that?" My voice has an anxious, peevish edge that I loathe.

Perhaps because he knows the question so well, perhaps because he knows the futility of the whole discussion, my father's face relaxes. He understands that he's never going to persuade me. He likes to give it his best shot, though. "Why search for what's already there? Why believe words can do more than they can do?"

I find myself searching for those words, not the ones that can do more than words can do, but the ones that will end our disputes, that will make my attachment clear as the early evening light coming through the living room window. The contemplative look on my father's face doesn't lessen my feelings. "I don't believe the words can do more than they can do. I believe the words can express part of what we are that otherwise wouldn't get expressed. I believe the words are the shadows we cast on the wall. I believe in those shadows." I never mean to get so worked up. Like a frat boy on Sunday morning, I shake my head as if to clear it.

When I play the card of what I believe, the strange ground I stand on, my father knows that the discussion is finished. He also knows it's not a discussion. It's more like two people hailing one another from opposite sides of a big river. When they try to speak across the water, their voices get lost. Those small human voices, however intent and harried and concerned, can't carry that far. Neither person walks away from the riverbank but neither communicates either. It's one of the mysteries, how children aren't replicates yet embody crucial pieces of their parents.

We switch to our long-standing, safe topics. We can talk baseball any time of the year. We can talk about how the global weather is changing.

We can talk about how the Mexicans have their heads on straighter than Americans. My dad is teaching himself Spanish from books and tapes. He doesn't have long to live but he's learning a new language. There's not much I can say about that without starting to cry. It's why I make these trips.

I can appreciate how poetry bugs people. It's a parallel universe to the one we are living in already. Who needs a parallel universe where language is so compressed and incisive and unpredictable? My dad spent his life with numbers and financial reports. Though he has his metaphors as in "cooked the books" and "bum rap," he's in favor of the straight-ahead. He's not in favor of young men killing themselves and leaving behind the ministrations that did not save them. He's not in favor of despair. Nor am I. I like the birds and the rain and the fish in my dad's tanks. In the darkest hour praise remains. That's hard to accept but it's beautiful, too.

Acknowledgments:

"1926" and "Robinson" are reprinted from *The Collected Poems of Weldon Kees,* edited by Donald Justice, by permission of the University of Nebraska Press. Copyright 1962, 1975 by the University of Nebraska Press. © renewed by the University of Nebraska Press.

"In Celebration of My Uterus" is from LOVE POEMS by Anne Sexton. Copyright © 1967, 1968, 1969 by Anne Sexton, renewed by Linda G. Sexton. Reprinted by permission of Houghton Mifflin Company. All rights reserved.

"Menstruation at Forty" is from LIVE OR DIE by Anne Sexton. Copyright © 1966 by Anne Sexton, renewed 1994 by Linda G. Sexton. Reprinted by permission of Houghton Mifflin Company. All rights reserved.

Joe Bolton's "Watching Bergman Films with My Father and "Elegy at Summer's End" are from *The Last Nostalgia: Poems, 1982-1990.* Copyright © 1999 by Ed Bolton. Reprinted with the permission of the University of Arkansas Press, www.uapress.com.

"Syracuse Airport" is from THE COLLECTED POEMS OF AUDRE LORDE by Audre Lorde. Copyright © 1997 by The Audre Lorde Estate. Used by permission of W. W. Norton & Company, Inc., and Charlotte Sheedy Literary Agency.

"Writ on the Eve of My 32nd Birthday" by Gregory Corso is from LONG LIVE MAN, copyright © 1962 by Gregory Corso. Reprinted by permission of New Directions Publishing Corp.

"Marriage" (excerpts) and "Poets Hitchhiking on the Highway" (excerpts) by Gregory Corso are from THE HAPPY BIRTHDAY OF DEATH, copyright © 1960 by New Directions Publishing Corp. Reprinted by permission of New

Books in the Notable Voices Series

The Poetry Life: Ten Stories, Baron Wormser
Surviving Has Made Me Crazy, Mark Nepo
Fun Being Me, Jack Wiler
Common Life, Robert Cording
Against Consolation, Robert Cording
To the Marrow, Robert Seder
The Origins of Tragedy & Other Poems, Kenneth Rosen
Apparition Hill, Mary Ruefle

Other Books by Baron Wormser

POETRY

The White Words (1983)
Good Trembling (1985)
Atoms, Soul Music and Other Poems (1989)
When (1997)
Mulroney and Others (2000)
Subject Matter (2004)
Carthage (2005)
Scattered Chapters: New and Selected Poems (2008)

PROSE

Teaching the Art of Poetry: The Moves (co-author, 2000)
A Surge of Language: Teaching Poetry Day by Day (co-author, 2004)
The Road Washes Out in Spring: A Poet's Memoir of Living Off the Grid (2006)

CavanKerry's Mission

Through publishing and programming, CavanKerry Press connects communities of writers with communities of readers. We publish poetry that reaches from the page to include the reader by the finest new and established contemporary writers. Our programming brings our books and our poets to people where they live, cultivating new audiences and nourishing established ones.